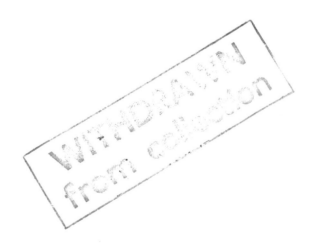

SHOOTING
FOR
BEGINNERS

Moulton College, West Street, Moulton, Northampton, NN3 7RR
Tel: 01604 673545 • Email: lrcenquiries@moulton.ac.uk

G3034 Designed by Learning Materials

SHOOTING
FOR
BEGINNERS

An Introduction
to the Sport

GRAHAM DOWNING

Quiller

To Becky, George and Sarah

Preface to Second Edition

Several significant developments have taken place in shooting since this book was first published, not least a new set of restrictive firearms legislation which has had an impact upon shooters of all sorts. However, there are also plenty of positive signs within the sport, and chief amongst these are the new initiatives by the shooting associations to encourage new entrants into shooting. These are having a welcome impact. Young people can now find much more guidance on how to get started, while the number of women shooters is currently showing a welcome increase. Driven game shooting is also becoming ever more accessible as the changing rural economy prompts more farmers to diversify into country sports.

I would like to thank all those who have commented on the revisions to this second edition, and most particularly I would like to thank my wife and family for their support and their enthusiastic companionship in the shooting field.

Graham Downing
Chediston, 2003

Copyright © 2003 Graham Downing

First published in the UK in 1996 by Swan Hill Press, an imprint of Quiller Publishing Ltd
Second Edition 2003
Reprinted 2004
Reprinted under the Quiller imprint 2009

British Library Cataloguing-in-Publication Data
A catalogue record for this book
is available from the British Library

ISBN 978 1 904057 31 4

The right of Graham Downing to be identified as the author of this work has been asserted in accordance with the Copyright, Design and Patent Act 1988

Printed in China

Quiller

An imprint of Quiller Publishing Ltd
Wykey House, Wykey, Shrewsbury, SY4 1JA
Tel: 01939 261616 Fax: 01939 261606
E-mail: info@quillerbooks.com
Website: www.countrybooksdirect.com

Contents

It is only too easy to think of education as a process of teaching young people about conventional academic subjects in schools. That is certainly a very important aspect, but to give education this exclusive quality is to imply that young people need no other instruction, or experience, to prepare them for adult life.

Academic and technical qualifications are certainly vital for economic success in an age of increasing technological sophistication, but that ignores the social and cultural values of intelligent participation in leisure activities.

As this comprehensive book makes quite clear, the sustainable exploitation of natural resources is possible provided traditional rules and customs are carefully observed. Properly managed shooting has never put any game species at risk of extinction, moreover, it has made a significant contribution to the conservation of the countryside and to the economy of rural areas - and continues to do so.

I am quite sure that this excellent book will help any number of people - young and not so young - to a better understanding of all that is meant by 'shooting'.

Introduction

Shooting is one of the most popular outdoor participant sports. In Britain some 750,000 people go shooting, and while a little more than a quarter of them concentrate solely on clay pigeon shooting, the remainder go out into the countryside to hunt live quarry, whether for sport or to control pests. In doing so they are following a tradition which traces its roots back hundreds of years, one which has played a major part in the creation of the landscape we see today.

Sporting shooting provides pleasure and satisfaction in a number of different ways. For the vast majority of us who live in towns and cities, it provides the opportunity to get out into the countryside, to enjoy the surroundings of fields, woods, moors and marshes and to exercise those hunting skills and instincts which are deep within all of us. In doing so we learn to appreciate and respect the countryside, its traditions and its way of life, while participating in an activity which is so

absorbing that it has the capacity to take our minds completely off the worries of the everyday world.

Some branches of the sport, like game shooting, involve meeting and mixing with other people, and the friendship and companionship which develops at the covertside or on the traditional farm shoot is enjoyed and appreciated by many. Other shooters pursue more solitary forms of the sport. The wildfowler on the lonely marshes at dawn and the pigeon shooter in his hide derive their pleasure from the challenge that comes from pitting their own wits against those of a truly wild quarry. They know that only when their hunting skills are honed to perfection are they likely to achieve success and come home with ducks, geese or woodpigeons in their game bags.

Yet others are absorbed by the relationship between man and his age-old hunting companion, the working dog. Handling, training and breeding gundogs requires endless patience and dedication, but the pleasure and satisfaction to be gained from forging a partnership with a working gundog is enormous. For many shooters, working their dog is a central part of the attraction of shooting, and indeed there are plenty who are quite happy to leave the gun at home and enjoy instead a day's beating with their spaniel or picking up with their retriever.

A further pleasure is that which is enjoyed around the dinner table, for with the exception of a very few birds or animals which are shot purely for the purposes of pest control, everything which the shooter brings home in his game bag provides wholesome and delicious food. Game birds, pigeons, wildfowl, rabbits and hares are low in fat and, because they have all fed on a rich and varied natural diet, they are full of flavour. Although in this country few people other than shooters and their families eat game, elsewhere in the world it is recognised widely as a luxury food and greatly sought after. As a result, there is a thriving export trade in such things as pheasants and woodpigeons.

This trade, which enables estates to sell what is surplus to their own needs, helps put large sums of money back into the rural economy. This, however, is only a small part of the economic benefit which shooting brings to Britain. Each year, millions of pounds are spent by shooters, many of them visitors from overseas, on their sport. This expenditure provides jobs for thousands of people, among them gamekeepers, hoteliers and those in the tourist industry, game farmers, sporting agents, those who sell and maintain four-wheel-drive vehicles and those who work in the gun trade. Britain's long tradition of making high-quality sporting guns is recognised and admired the world over, and the gun and cartridge trade which is supported by shooting sports in turn ensures that our gunmakers can continue to maintain Britain's reputation as a source of the finest sporting firearms.

At a national level, the economic impact of shooting may be modest. Locally, however, it can be very important indeed. Because shooting often takes place in remote parts of the country where there may be few other job opportunities outside forestry and farming, the employment generated by shooting can represent a lifeline to rural communities, one on which many people rely for a large part of their living. This is especially the case in Scotland.

Apart from helping to maintain rural communities, shooting also preserves the landscape and its wildlife. Traditionally, where farmers and landowners have been interested in shooting, they have created an attractive and diverse landscape with woods, hedgerows and wetlands which are favoured by game birds and animals. Country estates were very often laid out for shooting. Their landscapes, which are today admired and cherished, are still maintained in the traditional manner because of the sport which they provide. The shooting interest has played a large part in the saving of valuable landscape features from the pressures of intensive farming, and today many farmers are planting new coverts and spinneys for game. In addition, sporting farmers are among the leaders in the development of 'green' farming practices such as the creation of conservation headlands and field margins.

It is not just pheasants and partridges which benefit from the countryside management undertaken in the name of shooting. Wildlife of all sorts thrives in the rich and secure habitats which are created, from wild birds and mammals to butterflies and rare plants. This fact is well recognised by all the leading conservation agencies and voluntary bodies, some of which in turn rely on shooting groups such as wildfowling clubs to help supervise and protect their own wildlife reserves.

There is, however, a dilemma in many people's minds in that while shooting may well conserve some birds and animals, it directly causes the death of others. One cannot escape the fact that if you are planning to go shooting, then the consequence may well be that a pheasant, rabbit or duck is killed. It is therefore sometimes assumed that shooters damage wildlife, and that they are cruel and barbaric.

In fact shooters preserve far more wildlife than they destroy. While every hunter will go to great lengths to kill his quarry, his aim is only to harvest the natural increment which every quarry species produces each year. He will always want to ensure that there is plenty left to breed and reproduce in order that there may continue to be birds and animals to hunt in the future. This is known as the principle of 'wise use' of game.

Since the earliest times hunters have protected the creatures they pursue by imposing close seasons during the breeding period, and by restricting the ways in which birds or animals may be killed or taken. Such regulation has often distinguished sporting shooting from commercial hunting. While commercial hunters have been responsible for wiping out entire species, sporting shooters have been at pains to ensure that, although an individual animal may die in the course of the hunt, the species as a whole will survive and flourish. The crucial difference between the commercial hunter and the sportsman is that while the one derives economic benefit from the dead creature, whether from its hide or its meat, the other derives his 'benefit' or enjoyment from the hunt itself. He often sets self-imposed conditions which deliberately make it harder for him to kill his quarry. To the commercial hunter, returning empty-handed from a hunting trip represents economic loss; the true sportsman on the other hand accepts a blank day with equanimity. He is enriched as much by an 'unsuccessful' hunting trip as by one which results in a full game bag.

The charge of cruelty is often made by those who describe shooting as a 'bloodsport'. However, no shooter ever deliberately seeks to inflict cruelty, that is to say unnecessary suffering, on the birds or animals he shoots. The aim is always to kill cleanly and to avoid wounding, and most shooters ensure that they have with them a dog to quickly recover any quarry which is not killed outright by their shot. Very often a shooter will forgo the opportunity of taking further shots by spending time searching for a wounded bird or animal which he has lost. Nor is shooting barbaric. Indeed, it and the other hunting sports which preceded it have long existed as a part of many highly civilised societies, including our own. They have added richness and colour to literature, art and music and prompted the development of skills in science, technology and engineering, and they continue to do so today. Indeed, the field sports of hunting, shooting and fishing are the core around which complex cultures are based.

There remains, however, the question of whether it is right for the shooter to kill another creature in the course of what is essentially a recreational activity, and it is a question which everyone who shoots will at some time ask themselves. Before doing so, they should ponder the fact that life only exists by taking or exploiting other life. Those of us who rely upon other people, such as farmers, to produce the food we eat, the milk we drink or the wool and leather for our clothing and shoes merely delegate the act of exploiting or killing other animals to somebody else. There is nothing inherently wrong in that, of course. Farmers, on the whole, carry out their task with care and compassion, and to them the cycle of birth and death is part of everyday experience.

That natural cycle of birth and death, which is so much part of the countryside, is fundamental to life itself, and yet modern society has tended to divorce people from it. Not many of us can hope to become farmers. By taking part in field sports such as shooting, however, hundreds of thousands of people are able at least to start to get back in touch with the natural world.

Traditionally, most shooters have found their way into the sport because they have followed in the footsteps of their fathers, uncles or other family members or friends who have been keen shooters. If you have no family involvement in shooting or do not live in the countryside, it can often be very difficult to know how to take up the sport, however keen you are to do so.

In fact there are several common routes into shooting for the enthusiastic newcomer. One of the first ports of call for many people is a local shooting school, the address and telephone number of which can be obtained from the phone book or from one of the shooting associations. Here you can learn the art of handling a gun safely and competently under the guidance of a qualified instructor. Shooting successfully at artificial targets is an enormous confidence booster and an enjoyable form of the sport in its own right, as thousands of competitive clay pigeon shooters will testify. When you have honed your skills at clay pigeons, then the time may

come that you want to move on to sporting shooting in the field, and there are a number of ways in which this can be done.

If you are confident of your shooting skills, and absolutely sure of your ability to handle a gun safely, then there are plenty of shooting opportunities advertised in the shooting magazines. Shooting, whether it be for game, wildfowl or even woodpigeons, can be bought by the day or as part of a package provided by a hotel or guest house. Before booking, check to make sure that beginners are accepted, and that a 'loader' will be available to join you out game shooting or a guide will accompany you on your wildfowling or pigeon-shooting trip. Make it quite clear that you are a novice: nobody will think the worse of you for it and indeed, the overwhelming majority of shooters will be keen and eager to help you. In due course, and once you have made friends in the shooting field, you may wish to join a local game-shooting syndicate and thereby gain the opportunity to participate in a set number of shooting days each season, and perhaps also to invite one or more of your new-found shooting friends to join you.

Another route into shooting is to join a club. Pigeon-shooting and rough-shooting clubs exist all round the country, and wildfowling clubs control much of the finest wildfowl shooting around our coasts. They organise enjoyable social functions as well as renting or owning land for shooting. Most clubs run clay shoots during the summer, and as a member you will very often be expected to do your bit to assist with countryside management tasks, from building release pens to constructing bridges across a salt marsh. Shooting clubs offer a supportive environment for the novice shooter, and there will generally be members who will be prepared to offer advice and assistance, and to let you accompany them on their shooting trips. Most shooting clubs are affiliated to the British Association for Shooting and Conservation (BASC), from whom the name of the club secretary or chairman can be obtained.

There is also an increasing number of opportunities open to young shooters. All the national shooting associations, plus many local shooting clubs, hold special training and tuition days for young shots, normally at recognised clay pigeon shooting grounds. Generally guns and ammunition are provided, and expert tuition and guidance is always on hand. Young shooters' days do not merely provide instruction on shotgun handling. They combine practical shooting tuition with guidance on gun safety and other activities such as air rifle shooting. Details of nationally run instruction days for young shooters held during school holidays can be obtained from the BASC, the Countryside Alliance (CA) and the Game Conservancy Trust.

In addition, all these organisations hold courses for people of all ages on subjects connected with shooting. These range from shoot management and vermin control courses to gundog training days and wildfowling courses which provide the opportunity for participants to go shooting under the supervision of experienced wildfowlers.

Even if you do not shoot, there are plenty of opportunities to get involved in the shooting scene by offering your services to a local gamekeeper who is looking for beaters or who needs assistance with game rearing during the summer months. Gundog clubs are also ready to welcome new members who are interested in training their dogs for work in the shooting field. There are few better ways of understanding and learning to appreciate the sport than by getting involved in beating, shoot management and gundog work.

Finally, everyone who takes part in shooting or its associated activities should be a member of at least one of the national organisations which work on behalf of the sport. There are a number of membership bodies associated with shooting, but the three which are of most importance are the BASC, the CA and the Game Conservancy Trust. With 117,000 members, the BASC is the largest shooting organisation in Britain. It represents shooting interests at local, national and international level, and provides a wealth of advice and support to members through its technical departments and regional centres. The CA works on behalf of all field sports, including hunting, shooting, fishing, coursing and falconry. It is especially active in the fields of politics and public relations, and in combating those who seek to curtail or abolish the traditional sports of the countryside. The Game Conservancy Trust is a charitable organisation which devotes its efforts to research into game and its habitat. It undertakes a wide range of scientific work related to game birds and animals, and is respected worldwide as an authority on game and wildlife conservation. Linked to it is a commercial body, Game Conservancy Ltd, which provides shoot management advice and which runs courses. The names and addresses of these organisations can be found elsewhere in this book.

Whether you are just starting on your shooting career or are looking to develop and widen an established interest in shooting, remember that you do not need to look far to find an experienced shooter prepared to help and guide you in a sport which can provide lifelong interest and enjoyment.

Hunters with wheel-lock guns in 1582

CHAPTER 1
The History of Shooting

Since man first walked the earth, he has been a hunter. Long before human beings ever learned to grow crops and feed themselves and their families by farming the land, they obtained their food by gathering edible plants from the wild, by catching fish and by hunting birds and animals. Although today those of us who live in developed countries no longer need to hunt in order to survive, the hunting instinct remains deep within everyone. Pastimes like shooting, in which modern man can practise traditional hunting skills such as marksmanship, the use of working dogs and the pitting of human wits against those of his quarry, therefore satisfy a universal need.

Food is still a valuable by-product of hunting, as anyone who has had a meal of roast pheasant or venison will testify, but for many hundreds of years hunting in the developed world has been undertaken mainly because it is enjoyed as a sport or recreation, so just like every other sport it has developed a complicated code of rules and conventions. In many cases these rules serve to emphasise the importance of hunting skills and the hunter's respect for his quarry. They tip the balance in favour of the hunted bird or animal and make the taking or killing of it more difficult, rendering the successful hunt more rewarding and satisfying in consequence. For example you will never see a pheasant shooter take a shot at a sitting pheasant. In fact the faster it is flying and the further away it is from him – provided that it is still within range of

his gun – the better he likes it. If his object were simply to kill pheasants he would be far better off shooting them on the ground with a rifle; but it is not. Instead the modern shooter's main object is to achieve the satisfaction that comes when a sporting shot has been well executed.

Perhaps ancient hunters, at the earliest stages of man's development, also appreciated the excitement of the hunt and the satisfaction which it gave them. Even if they did, however, their main priority must have been to kill sufficient game to guarantee the survival of themselves and their families.

Hunting in ancient times

Early man soon developed highly complex hunting cultures. Indeed, it is widely accepted that hunting contributed greatly to the development of co-operation between different groups of ancient people, and so became one of the cornerstones of emerging civilisation. To hunt large and dangerous animals like the cave bear, which was extensively pursued in the Old Stone Age or Paleolithic era, needed teamwork and co-operation between individual hunters. This requirement almost certainly helped to develop the power of language and communication. Hunting also led to the establishment of ritual. Neanderthal hunters living 170,000 years ago in what is now Austria developed a cult in which their quarry, the bear, became an

A wildfowler with a matchlock in around 1570. Matchlocks were the first effective hunting weapons.

object of religious significance, and late Paleolithic hunters living between 12,000 and 20,000 years ago decorated the walls and roofs of their caves with magnificent pictures of the animals they hunted. The most famous paintings at the Altamira and Lascaux caves, in Spain and France respectively, and the newly discovered ones at Chauvet near Avignon were probably connected with rituals aimed at ensuring the success of future hunting expeditions, and must certainly have been central to the developing cultures of the communities of people who created them.

Ancient man used several methods to kill his quarry. Spears, traps of all sorts and trained hunting dogs were among the first to appear, and then in the Neolithic period came the bow and arrow. For the first time, hunters had the means to shoot accurately at and kill distant and even fast-moving birds and animals.

These basic tools – the spear, the trap, the hound and the bow and arrow – remained central to hunting for thousands of years, to be joined in due course by trained birds of prey.

The birth of firearms

The invention of gunpowder some time before 1200 was one of the most momentous events in the history of man. Nobody knows exactly who discovered that the mixing of charcoal, saltpetre and sulphur created a powerful explosive, or where the mixture was first made. However, it seems that gunpowder was being used in China for making fireworks long before it was known in the West. The first European to be credited with the manufacture of gunpowder was the Franciscan friar Roger Bacon, who wrote down the precious formula in about 1250. Before very long, the possibilities of using gunpowder as a propellant had become apparent, and primitive mortars shaped like flower vases were used by the armies of the day to launch rocks and other projectiles at enemy positions.

The earliest hand gun, a simple tube closed at one end and mounted on a stick or haft, appeared in the fourteenth century. Though useful as a weapon of war, it was not much good for hunting. It was clumsy and could not be aimed with any accuracy, and in any case firing it by means of a smouldering 'match' – a long piece of glowing cord – was such a complex and uncertain process that most birds or animals would have been able to make good their escape long before the shooter could get anywhere near them to discharge his piece. The bow, the hound and the hawk held sway for another 200 years before a crucial modification to the basic design of the gun finally enabled aimed shots to be taken with accuracy and some degree of consistency.

WHAT IS GUNPOWDER?

An explosive is a mixture or compound which burns very rapidly and produces a very large volume of gas. All explosives must therefore combine a highly combustible substance with a chemical which produces the necessary oxygen to allow combustion to take place. Gunpowder, which was probably developed in China and the Islamic world long before it became known in Europe, is one of the simplest explosives and consists of saltpetre (potassium nitrate), charcoal and sulphur. When the mixture is ignited, the charcoal and sulphur burn in the oxygen given off by the saltpetre, and the gunpowder produces about 4,000 times its own volume of gas, plus a great deal of choking grey smoke.

Gunpowder was originally made in private homes, but the dangers involved in this practice were soon recognised, and in 1461 its manufacture was limited to special places such as the Tower of London. Eventually gunpowder factories were developed. Because of the ever-present risk of explosion these were built far away from human habitation.

Powered by water, they utilised wooden machinery to reduce the risk of accidental ignition.

'Black powder', as gunpowder is now called in order to distinguish it from modern propellants, is a black granular substance, which is supplied in varying degrees of coarseness to users of antique or reproduction muzzle loading guns. The finer grades burn more quickly and are used in pistols and for priming large guns. Sporting guns require a medium grade, of the consistency of coarse sand. Large guns and cannons use a slower burning coarse grain powder, in which the grains measure 2–3 mm across.

Whatever the grain size, black powder burns relatively slowly and progressively, giving a 'gentle shove' up the barrel rather than a 'big kick'. It therefore develops much lower pressures in the chamber than the nitro powders which were developed in the later nineteenth century. Old guns which have been proved only for black powder must never be used with modern cartridges.

The matchlock

This development was the creation of the matchlock gun, which had two important features. One was the fact that the firing tube – the barrel – was mounted on a stock that could be held against the shoulder or cheek, thus enabling the shooter to sight along the top of it. The other was that the means of ignition, the slow-burning match, was clamped in a curved metal arm call a 'serpentine' which in turn was operated by a lever or trigger. This enabled the match to be applied in a controlled way by the fingers of one hand to a priming pan containing a small quantity of gunpowder. When the powder in the priming pan ignited, it sent a hot spurt of flame through a touch-hole directly into the main powder charge, thus firing the gun.

For the first time, deliberate shots could be taken at game birds or animals, provided that the shooter was able to stalk within range, and it was not long before the matchlock gun developed to a high degree of sophistication. These guns were elaborate and costly, so they were available only to the wealthier classes of society. But is was clear that the idea of stalking game, and more particularly wild-fowl, had taken hold amongst the common people, for in 1533 Henry VIII passed an Act which forbade anyone to shoot with any handgun unless he had land worth £100 a year, a great deal of money in those days. Henry, himself a shooting enthusiast, was obviously concerned to restrict the new sport to the better off, and to ensure that the menfolk of England did not neglect the prac-tice of archery with their longbows, a skill which in that period was of vital importance to the nation in time of war.

Firearms were not so easily put down, however, and early gunmakers eagerly sought to improve their products. Particular atten-tion was paid to the means of ignition, for the slow-burning match was by no means ideal. In wet or windy weather the glowing cord would all too easily be extinguished, and if a matchlock was used for hunting game, the burning match would frequently alert the quarry to the shooter's presence.

Early ignition systems such as this wheel-lock in a picture from 1624 required the hunter to stalk to within range of his quarry. Here a hunter uses his horse to help him approach waterfowl.

The wheel-lock

The first mechanical means of igniting a firearm came with the invention of the wheel-lock. This employed a clockwork system which was used to drive a mechanism rather like the one which can be found in a modern cigarette lighter. At the centre of the wheel-lock was a serrated steel wheel, which could be made to spin round when the trigger was pressed. A piece of iron pyrites, held in the jaws of a 'cock', was forced against the fast-revolving wheel, sending a shower of sparks into the priming pan and so firing the gun.

Although wheel-locks became popular in Germany and eastern Europe, where a robust version known as the *tschinke* was developed to withstand rough handling in the field, it never achieved wide acceptance in England. The main reason for this was that it was a very complex, delicate and thus expensive piece of engineering. It was also one that was largely unsuited to the demands of the hunter. So it remained principally a weapon of war and more particularly a tool of the mounted soldier. Most everyday people stuck with their old-fashioned matchlocks, and after the English Civil War of the 1640s large numbers of matchlocks came into circulation and were widely used by hunters to shoot game and wildfowl.

Flint and steel

Meanwhile, gunmakers were constantly on the lookout for new methods of ignition, and eventually they turned to flint and steel to fire their weapons. The earliest form of flintlock, known as the 'snaphance' after the Dutch word *snaphaan* or snapping cock, appeared in the middle of the sixteenth century. It had a cock containing a flint, which struck a moving steel or 'frizzen'. To operate his snaphance, the shooter first had to slide the cover off the priming pan and ensure that the frizzen was set and the cock drawn fully back. When he pulled the trigger, the flint struck the frizzen, which moved smartly backwards allowing the sparks to fall into the open pan.

This was certainly an advance on the old wheel-lock, but it still required the shooter to open the priming pan manually before he fired, so exposing the priming powder to

The advent of the flintlock enabled sportsmen to shoot flying quarry.

wind and weather and preventing the taking of anything but slow, deliberate shots. That all changed with the invention of the true flintlock in the first quarter of the seventeenth century. In the flintlock, the frizzen and pan cover were joined together into an L-shaped component which flipped back when it was struck a glancing blow by the flint, opening the pan to receive its hail of hot sparks, and so allowing the gun to be fired.

For 200 years the flintlock reigned supreme. Gunmakers across Europe developed and perfected it into a weapon which was both elegantly engineered and beautiful to look at. In fact the lines of the later flintlock are broadly similar to those of the modern sporting gun, and the age of the flintlock saw the birth of famous gunmaking firms, some of which are still in business today. The flintlock was reasonably weatherproof, easy to load and fire, pretty reliable provided that it was kept clean and the flint regularly replaced, and most importantly, it offered much faster ignition than any system which preceded it. This meant that for the first time shooters had a real chance of being able to shoot birds in flight. Until this time shooting had been an activity undertaken largely by ordinary people who stalked and killed birds for food, while the upper classes stuck mostly to their hounds and hawks. With the arrival of *pteryplegia* or wing-shooting, there was renewed interest in shooting amongst all classes of society and suddenly it became an accepted and recognisable sport in its own right.

When a flintlock is fired, however, there is still an appreciable delay between the moment the trigger is pulled, the ignition of the priming pan, and the point at which the main charge goes off, thus sending the shot out of the barrel. This means that a great deal of forward allowance has to be given when taking a crossing shot. Sportsmen thus concentrated on walking-up their quarry over pointing dogs. When flushed, the game would normally offer a going-away shot, to which the flintlock was well suited.

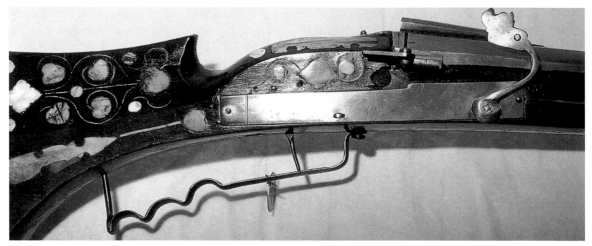

Flemish or German matchlock musket from around 1610.

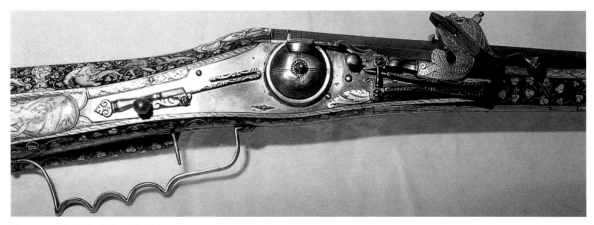

German wheel-lock from 1614.

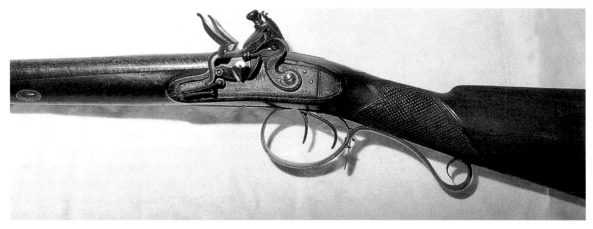

An English flintlock at the peak of its development. This double-barrelled gun was made by the famous gunsmith Henry Nock in 1805. Its design sets the standard for successive generations of sporting shotguns.

A double-barrelled percussion shotgun by Redfern, with brass powder flask, leather shot pouch and percussion cap dispenser.

The percussion system

The next great revolution in gunmaking occurred in 1807, when a Scottish clergyman called Alexander Forsyth patented a means of firing a gun by using a detonating powder. This was a chemical compound which exploded when a small quantity of it was struck a direct blow. Although it caused too violent an explosion for it to be suitable for use as a propellant, it was found to be a perfect alternative to flint and steel in igniting a conventional charge of gunpowder. At first Forsyth's invention was dismissed by conservative shooters, who preferred to stick to their trusty flintlocks. But before long, the benefits of the detonating system became obvious. In particular, it was much more reliable than the flintlock in wet weather, when the old-fashioned flint and steel was particularly prone to misfiring. So before long, gunmakers rushed to develop the best way of

applying the detonating principle to the sporting gun. By the time that Forsyth's patent expired in 1821, the true percussion shotgun was born.

Instead of the side-mounted priming pan of the flintlock, the standard percussion shotgun has a small tube or 'nipple' which leads directly down into the chamber, where the powder charge is located. A small copper cap, containing a tiny quantity of detonating material, is placed over the top of the nipple. When struck by the hammer of the gun this sends a jet of very hot flame straight into the centre of the powder, thereby igniting it evenly and quickly. The percussion shotgun reigned supreme for 20 years, and vast numbers of these guns were made, while many flintlocks were also converted to the new system. Percussion shotguns remained popular for even longer in the expanding colonies of the European powers, and it was well into the twentieth century before they finally disappeared from the gunmakers' catalogues.

Breech-loading guns

The reason for their passing was the next great leap forward in firearms technology, the development of the breech-loading gun. For 500 years, gunmakers had developed ever more sophisticated ignition systems, but they had largely failed to address the fact that guns still had to be loaded from the muzzle. Nineteenth-century shooters had to tip powder, wadding and shot down the muzzles of their guns, and drive the charge home with a ramrod just as generations of their forebears had done. But muzzle-loading is a slow and at times uncertain process. Even the most experienced shooter could not expect to get off more than three shots a minute at the very most, and there was always the risk that in the heat of the moment an unfired barrel might have a second charge rammed down on top of the first, with disastrous consequences. Equally, the shooter had to handle gunpowder in bulk, and even when it was contained in a specially designed powder flask there was still the chance that a glowing ember in a newly fired gun could ignite the stream of fresh powder trickling down the barrel as the shooter reloaded, causing the flask to blow up in his hand.

Ingenious gunmakers therefore turned their attention to developing a method of loading a gun from the breech with a cartridge containing both powder and shot. The first breech-loading system to achieve widespread success was the pinfire system, in which the cartridge was fitted with a projecting pin which, when the gun was closed, stuck out of a small aperture against the face of the breech. When the trigger was pulled, a hammer drove the pin sharply into the cartridge and detonated the charge.

The pinfire system enjoyed only brief popularity following the Great Exhibition of 1851 where it was first put on public display, and within ten years the centre-fire cartridge had been developed. The centre-fire system employed a cartridge which had the detonating primer fitted to its base, and it was fired by means of a hammer which struck a firing pin or striker passing through a hole in the face of the breech. This system has been refined but not bettered, and it remains in general use today.

For a while, sporting shotguns continued to use external hammers, and indeed, the 'hammer gun' can still be seen in use today. One of its benefits is that because the hammers have to be drawn back or 'cocked' before the gun is fired, it is plain to see when the gun is in the ready-to-fire condition. Likewise when the hammers are at rest, the gun is seen to be relatively safe. But using a hammer gun also has disadvantages. It is necessary to cock both hammers before you can shoot, and this takes time, even for the most practised shooter. Hammers can also get caught in twigs or barbed wire, which can cause the gun to discharge accidentally. So in the 1880s, gunmakers brought in the 'hammerless' gun in which the hammers were removed from the outside of the action and instead were incorporated into the internal firing mechanism. No longer was there any need to draw the hammers back by hand, and in most hammerless guns, the action is cocked automatically when the barrels are opened for reloading.

The nineteenth century, a period which saw more changes and developments in firearms technology than any other, also brought with it the introduction of mass production. For the first time it became possible to replace expensive and time-consuming hand labour with machine manufacture, thus opening up the way to the production of cheaper guns. A significant step was the replacement of traditional hand-forged 'Damascus' barrels – made by winding thin strips of red-hot metal around a cylindrical bar or mandrel and then forge-welding them into a tube – with barrels machine-drilled from solid bars of steel, such as we have today.

Spurred on by the rapidly developing market for sporting firearms both at home

and in the colonies, gunmakers worked feverishly on every conceivable idea in order to perfect the shotgun. Further refinements swiftly followed, such as the introduction of an ejector mechanism to expel the spent cartridge cases from the breech, and the development of the single trigger which could, if required, be used to replace the conventional double triggers on a double-barrelled gun. By the dawn of the twentieth century, the evolution of the sporting shotgun as we know it today was virtually complete.

New propellants

Alongside the development of the shotgun ran that of the explosive propellant which was used in it. We have seen how the recipe for gunpowder, or 'black powder' as it is known, was written down in the middle of the thirteenth century. Early powder was crude and unreliable. It burned slowly, and so a significant amount of time was needed from the moment of ignition to the point at which the powder charge developed its full pressure. Because of this, early guns had very long barrels to accommodate the progressive combustion of the propellant. By the end of the eighteenth century, the manufacture of black powder had developed into a fine art. It was made commercially in special water-powered powder mills, where the risk of explosion could be kept to an absolute minimum. But black powder still remained a messy explosive to use. In particular, it left large quantities of sulphurous black fouling behind after it was fired and produced great clouds of grey smoke. Soon, industrial chemists were busy at work finding alternatives.

Their searches centred around the new 'nitro' compounds which are formed when cellulose material such as cotton is treated with nitric acid. Pioneers like Alfred Nobel eventually formulated explosive materials which were stable and safe enough for use in firearms, and before long the dirty, smoky black powder gave way to the smokeless, fast-burning nitro powders we use today.

In 700 years, thanks to the ingenuity of countless gunmakers, the primitive 'hand-gonne' which was probably just as dangerous to its user as to its intended target, has been transformed into the sleek, elegant sporting shotgun we know today. Shooting has been made safe and efficient, while the mass manufacture of shotguns has brought the sport within reach of millions of people.

The percussion shotgun was fired by a copper cap containing a tiny quantity of detonating compound.

A pinfire shotgun by William Lowe, and cartridges. Note that protruding out of the base of the cartridges are brass pins, which were struck by the flattened hammers. The pinfire was the first widely successful breech loading system.

A double-barrelled 12-bore hammer gun. Guns of this type achieved universal popularity.

CHAPTER 2
Shotguns and Cartridges

Whether you wish to shoot game or clay pigeons, whether you want to pursue wild-fowl on the salt marsh, woodpigeons on the fields at harvest time or grouse on the moors, you will require a shotgun.

What is a shotgun? Put quite simply, it is a weapon designed to shoot a charge of small pellets, normally at a moving target. Every aspect of its construction is geared towards helping the shooter place an even and consistent pattern of shot on his selected target time and time again. At the heart of the shotgun is a powerful spring which works the lock, and which is compressed when the gun is cocked. This normally happens when the barrels are dropped down for loading. Pulling the trigger releases the spring, which drives the striker forward to make contact with the cartridge. The primer is ignited and in an instant the powder charge contained within the cartridge explodes, shooting the wad and shot up the barrel ahead of a rapidly expanding column of hot gases.

Lock, stock and barrel

A shotgun is described as a smooth-bored weapon. This means that unlike a rifle, which has a series of spiral grooves down its barrel to impart a steadying spin to the bullet, it has barrel walls which are absolutely smooth. Look through the barrel of an empty shotgun and you will see that the inside is highly polished. This ensures that any damage or distortion caused to the shot pellets as they travel up the tube is kept to an absolute minimum. Perfectly spherical pellets fly straight and true through the air; damaged ones do not, and so decrease the shooter's chance of killing his quarry or breaking his clay target. That is why many shotgun cartridges are fitted with a plastic wad containing a shot cup which gives further protection to the pellets as they are fired.

The 'action' of a shotgun is that section which contains most of the working parts that enable the gun to be cocked and fired. Like the barrel, the action is finely and carefully engineered to withstand the shock of the enormous pressures which are generated when the gun is fired. Fitted to the action is the stock, traditionally made of walnut, which enables the shooter to mount the gun snugly to his shoulder.

Apart from 'lock, stock and barrel', there are a number of fundamental parts or working controls to be found on the conventional shotgun. Below the barrels is the fore-end, which may contain within it those working parts which operate the ejector mechanism, designed to throw spent cartridges clear of the breech automatically when the gun is opened. When the fore-end is detached, the barrels can be removed easily from the stock and action.

Most modern shotguns are opened, or 'broken', by means of a top lever, to be found on top of the action. When it is pushed smartly to the right, the barrels drop down to enable the gun to be loaded. Immediately behind the top lever can usually be found the safety catch. This locks the triggers and prevents the gun from being fired, although the safety catch should never be relied upon, and no gun is ever 'safe' unless it is unloaded. Beneath the action will be found the trigger or triggers. A single-barrelled gun will obviously have only one trigger, but a double-barrelled gun may have either one or two. If there is only one trigger, then the gun may in addition be fitted with a selector button to enable the shooter to choose which barrel he wishes to fire first. If there are two triggers, then the front one normally operates the right barrel and the back one the left barrel. Around the triggers is a curved trigger guard to prevent them from being snagged and the gun fired accidentally.

Different types of shotgun

The ingenuity and inventiveness of generations of gunmakers and the demands of sportsmen for ever better weapons has led to the development of an almost bewildering variety of shotguns. To the collector or the firearms enthusiast the study of shotguns and the appreciation of their engineering and artistry can become a lifelong study. Yet there is a number of distinct types which every shooter will recognise.

Best known is the double-barrelled side-by-side shotgun. So called because the two barrels sit next to each other, the side-by-side has enjoyed over 200 years of popularity, and has long been favoured by the best English gunmakers. It is closely associated with game shooting, and until quite recently the guest turning up at a smart driven day with anything other than a side-by-side shotgun would have been given some very funny looks. Thankfully today's attitudes have changed and allow the shooter more freedom in his choice of shotgun than was once the case.

Within the broad class of side-by-side shotguns there are two further classifications which must be mentioned. At the quality end of the market is the sidelock, so called because the locks are mounted independently on side plates fitted to the sides of the action. The 'best' sidelock is the epitome of fine gunmaking. Its side plates form a magnificent canvas upon which the master engraver can practise his craft, while its thoroughbred lines, its balance and its exquisite artistry mark it out as a thing of beauty. But such a gun has a price tag to match, and a quality sidelock shotgun, hand built to the customer's measurements and specifications by a top London gunmaker, can cost £30,000 and take over two years to make.

The boxlock shotgun has a simpler mechanism with fewer component parts, and so is cheaper to make than the sidelock. Nevertheless, many good gunmakers have produced very fine boxlock shotguns over the years, and a well-built boxlock, made with care and precision from quality materials, will still last several lifetimes. Indeed, the boxlock design has changed little since the 1890s, and there are many such guns in regular use today which are more than 100 years old.

Rapidly increasing in popularity amongst shooters is the over-and-under shotgun. This design has the two barrels superimposed one on top of the other, producing a narrow sighting plane which improves the 'pointability' of the gun. Guns with superimposed barrels have been produced in small numbers by Europe's gunmakers for centuries, but it was the widespread adoption of the over-and-under shotgun by sport shooters in the United States which led to its present revival. The over-and-under is universally used by clay pigeon shooters, and in the world of game shooting its popularity is fast outstripping that of the more traditional side-by-side shotgun.

Single-barrelled shotguns are widely used in all forms of sporting shooting and, like their double-barrelled cousins, come in a variety of different forms. Perhaps the simplest is the basic break-action shotgun, which has been the workhorse of generations of gamekeepers, rough shooters and young shots. Cheap, rugged and reliable, the single-barrelled weapon is often selected as a first shotgun for the novice, and very good it is too, despite its obvious shortcomings.

Most shotguns in regular use today are hammerless. This means that the striker, or firing mechanism, is enclosed within the body of the action. Occasionally, however, one may come across guns with external hammers, known as hammer guns. These were universally used before the perfection of the hammerless action in the 1880s. Although it will usually be quite old, a hammer gun may be of very high quality, and some examples are greatly sought after by collectors. Using a hammer gun requires extra care, and since many were built before the advent of modern propellants, the proof marks of a hammer gun should always be checked to ensure that it is suitable for use with modern cartridges.

The bolt action is more widely associated with rifles than with shotguns. Nevertheless, the single-shot bolt-action principle can readily be adapted to shotgun manufacture, and very large numbers of bolt-action shotguns are in use, especially in the smaller calibres such as the .410 or 'four-ten'. To load a bolt-action shotgun, a cartridge is slid into the open breech, after which the bolt is pushed forwards and locked with a downward rotation of the bolt lever. After firing the cycle is reversed, the bolt lever being pushed upwards and the bolt drawn back to expel the empty cartridge case. Although it is essentially a simple system, effective operation of the bolt action requires practice, and it is not an ideal gun for the beginner.

A further category of single-barrelled shotguns is the magazine shotgun, which has the ability to fire multiple shots without further cartridges being introduced manually into the chamber. This category includes both the pump action and the semi-automatic shotgun.

A semi-automatic shotgun in use. The gun has just been fired and the spent cartridge case can be seen as it is thrown clear of the chamber.

Pump-action shotguns have a cylindrical magazine situated below the barrel. After a shot has been fired, a single back-and-forth pumping motion of the fore-end ejects the spent cartridge case, loads a fresh round into the chamber and cocks the gun at the same time. In a semi-automatic, the process of feeding a round from the magazine into the chamber is done automatically, by utilising either the propellant gases or the recoil from the preceding shot. All the shooter has to do is to pull the trigger.

Because they do not have to be broken for reloading, magazine shotguns are particularly popular amongst woodpigeon shooters and wildfowlers who shoot from confined hides. And because part of its recoil energy is used to work the reloading mechanism, the semi-automatic has a particularly low sensible recoil and is thus favoured by young shots and women shooters.

However, particular care must be taken with magazine shotguns, because when one is shooting in company one cannot break the

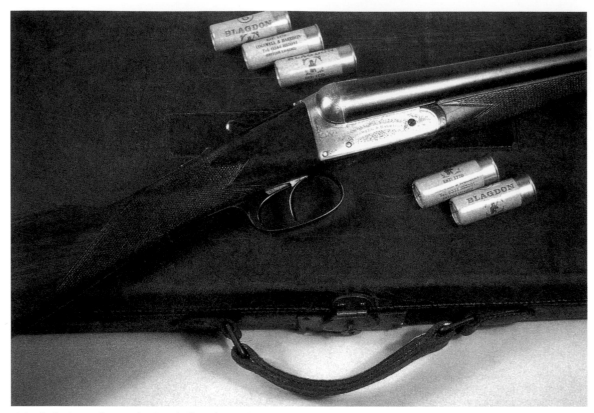

A boxlock ejector shotgun by Cogswell and Harrison. Though dating from 1889, this gun is in every respect the conventional sporting shotgun which one would expect to use in the shooting field today.

The over-and-under shotgun is widely used in many branches of sporting shooting.

gun as with a conventional break-action weapon to demonstrate to other shooters that it is unloaded and thus safe. For this reason, magazine shotguns are not favoured when shooting in the company of other people. In addition, their value is restricted by the law which states that they may hold no more than two rounds in the magazine in addition to one in the chamber. This gives the shooter no more than three shots before he has to reload.

This pair of sidelock ejector shotguns by the celebrated makers Holland and Holland represents the very peak of perfection in gunmaking.

A bolt action .410 shotgun, popular as a tool for pest control.

Shotgun calibres

Whereas rifle calibres are normally measured in millimetres or fractions of an inch, shotguns are gauged by bore size. Bore sizes hark back to the days when smooth-bore guns were used to fire single lead musket balls, and the number of the bore size corresponds to the number of balls of pure lead, each exactly fitting the bore of the gun, which together weigh 1 lb (453 g). Thus a perfectly spherical ball of lead weighing 1 oz (28 g), or $\frac{1}{16}$ lb, will fit exactly into a 16-bore barrel. Likewise, a ball weighing $\frac{1}{12}$ lb will fit a 12-bore. The higher the number of the bore size, therefore, the smaller its dimension.

By far the most popular size worldwide is the 12-bore. However, young shots and women shooters often prefer the smaller 20- or even 28-bore shotguns, with their light shot loads and consequently lower recoil. The less frequently encountered 16-bore is a halfway house between the 20 and the 12, and has its small band of strong supporters, especially elsewhere within the European Union. At the other end of the scale, the large-bore shotguns comprise the 10-bore, the 8-bore and the massive 4-bore. Such guns are rarely encountered outside the specialised field of wildfowling and in particular goose shooting, where they are used to deliver large charges of heavy shot at extreme range.

Two small and commonly encountered shotgun gauges are measured like rifle calibres in inches or millimetres. The .410 is valuable for vermin control and is a traditional calibre for children learning to shoot. However, the very small charge of shot which it is capable of firing makes it useful only at ranges of up to about 25 m, and consistent success with a .410 calls for very accurate marksmanship. In truth, the young newcomer to shooting is better off moving directly to one of the larger calibres, such as the 28-bore or, if he can manage it, the 20-bore. Smaller even than the .410 is the 9 mm or 'Number 3 garden gun'. This is useful for dealing with small vermin such as rats or mice in confined spaces, but it has no value as a sporting weapon.

Cartridges

Just as there is a very wide range of shotguns available to the sporting shooter, so the variety of cartridges appears almost limitless. However, the basic design of the centre-fire shotgun cartridge is extremely simple. A cartridge in essence contains three things: an explosive powder together with a means of ignition, a wad column to act as a piston, and a charge of shot. The expertise of ballisticians and cartridge manufacturers has refined these ingredients to the point at which a different cartridge is now available for just about any type of shooting.

The propellent powder – gunpowder has long been replaced by smokeless powders of various sorts – is ignited by the primer which sits in its own small chamber in the base of the cartridge. When hit by the striker, the primer directs a hot burst of flame into the powder charge, which has to burn cleanly and uniformly to accelerate the shot out of the barrel. A variety of powders exists, enabling the cartridge manufacturer to design loads which give the shot everything from a short, hard kick to a relatively long, slow push up the barrel.

Seated on top of the powder, the wad has a vital role to perform in transferring the energy of the propellant to the shot charge. Traditionally, wads were cut from thick organic felt or fibrous material, but in recent years the plastic monowad has been almost universally adopted. The monowad contains a shot cup which, as we have seen, protects the shot from abrasion against the barrel wall and thus helps to ensure that a better, more even pattern of shot strikes the target. However, plastic monowads have two major disadvantages in that they do not easily biodegrade and they cannot easily be picked up by hand like spent cartridge cases. Where a great deal of shooting takes place, a build-up of spent plastic monowads can occur, which both looks unsightly and can prove dangerous to grazing farm animals. For this reason, many clay pigeon grounds and some game shoots require the use of the traditional fibre wad.

Shot size

Shot comes in a variety of different sizes, from the smallest conventional size 9 (2 mm) to LG (9.1 mm) shot which is used against heavy game such as wild boar. The lower the number, the larger the shot size, and the most commonly used sizes are 4, 5, 6 and 7. For pheasants, partridges and other game birds, most shooters prefer sizes 6 and 7. The slightly larger size 5 is often preferred for use against rabbits, and for shooting hares or wildfowl size 4 can be very effective. Goose shooters use even larger shot sizes, such as 3, 1 or BB, while at the other end of the scale, specialist snipe shooters opt for size 8. The standard game load for a 12-bore shotgun is 30 g ($1^1/_{16}$ oz) of size 6 shot, containing 287 pellets.

Most shot used for shooting upland game is made from lead. However, some birds, especially waterfowl, can be at risk of lead poisoning when they eat spent lead pellets from areas which are regularly shot over. The problem has been highlighted by international bird protection treaties and in many parts of Europe and America legislation has been introduced which requires shooters to use non-toxic shot when shooting over important wetlands and when shooting wildfowl. Environmental Protection regulations introduced in 1999 extended this legislation to England and Wales. Scotland is also considering introducing regulations requiring non-toxic shot for waterfowl shooting.

Chamber length

The shotgun cartridge is contained in a tubular case which is fitted with a rimmed metal head. The case is normally made from plastic. Empty cartridge cases, like plastic wads, can cause a litter problem if they are not carefully picked up by the shooter. However, it is sometimes very difficult to find every last spent cartridge case, which is why some shooters still prefer to use paper cased cartridges which are biodegradable.

Since the outside diameter of the cartridge case is of necessity larger than the diameter of the wad which it contains, and since the wad has to fit snugly inside the barrel to prevent the propellant gases from escaping past it, it therefore follows that the cartridge is slightly wider than the bore size of the gun it is designed for. This means that a space must be created inside the breech end of the barrel to accommodate the thickness of the cartridge case. This space is known as the chamber. Different guns may have different chamber lengths, and it is very important when matching a cartridge to a particular gun that the cartridge which you choose is not longer than the chamber will allow. Although it may be possible to load a longer cartridge into the chamber, when it is fired dangerously high gas pressures may result. Standard 12-bore chamber lengths are 65 mm (2½ in) and 70 mm (2¾ in). Some wildfowling guns designed for long-range shooting are chambered for 'magnum' 75 mm (3 in) cartridges. A 65 mm cartridge may be used in a 70 mm chambered gun, but the reverse is not true: a 70 mm cartridge should never be used in a gun which has chambers of less than 70 mm.

Shotgun range

Many people are surprised that a shotgun, which normally has a much larger calibre than a rifle, cannot shoot nearly as far. In fact the shotgun is a very short-range weapon. The maximum effective range of a 12-bore shotgun is traditionally reckoned to be 40 yards (36m), and under normal shooting

SHOT SIZE AND TYPE

Lead is a soft grey metal which is relatively cheap and abundant and which has a high specific gravity of 11.34, making it ideally suited to the production of projectiles for use in guns. Lead melts at a temperature of only 327 degrees Celsius, and small shot is manufactured by allowing the liquid metal to pour through a sieve. As the droplets fall, they form into small spheres, which harden into pellets. These are graded according to size and dusted with a lubricant, normally powdered graphite.

Sometimes other metals are alloyed with the lead to make the shot harder and so reduce the risk of damage to the pellets as they are fired from a gun, ensuring a more even pattern. Lead shot may also be coated with metals like copper or nickel to improve performance in high-velocity, long range loads, and it may be used in combination with a granulated polymer 'buffering' powder, which reduces friction and crushing between individual pellets within the charge.

Non-lead shot has been required for use over wetlands and for wildfowl shooting in England and Wales since 1999. Several different types are available, the cheapest of which is 'steel' shot, which is in fact made of soft iron. Steel shot has been used by waterfowl shooters in the United States for several years and is now popular amongst UK wildfowlers. However, it has a lower specific gravity than lead, and this means that a larger pellet size must be used in order to maintain equivalent down-range striking energy. Other non-toxic alternatives such as bismuth and tungsten matrix are more expensive, but match the specific gravity of lead much more closely. They are particularly popular amongst users of traditional lightweight European guns.

Small shot is graded by numbers, but larger shot sizes are identified by letters. The most common lettered shot is BB, which is used for goose shooting, and is particularly popular in large bore guns. Other countries use differing shot size classifications, so it is necessary to take care when you buy foreign loaded cartridges. Some non-toxic shot cartridges are sold with the diameter of the shot marked in millimetres. Again, check the carton carefully.

SHOT SIZES

		Diameter				Diameter	
		mm	in			mm	in
●	LG	9.1	.36	●	3	3.3	.13
●	SG	8.4	.33	●	4	3.1	.12
●	Spec SG	7.6	.30	●	5	2.8	.11
●	SSG	6.8	.27	●	6	2.6	.10
●	AAA	5.2	.20	●	7	2.4	.095
●	BB	4.1	.16	●	7½	2.3	.09
●	1	3.6	.14	●	8	2.2	.085
				●	9	2.0	0.8

conditions, most shots will be taken at nearer 25 m. Even the very large-bore guns used by goose shooters are not effective at much over 50 m, and if he is to hit targets at that range time after time, the user of such a gun must be a very good shot indeed.

A shotgun kills by combining the infliction of damage to vital organs, such as the heart or lungs, with the shock of a multiple strike of pellets. To kill a particular quarry consistently, the shooter therefore has to ensure that sufficient pellets hit the target on every occasion, and that they have enough energy to cause that shock and vital damage. That in itself dictates the effective range of a shotgun and cartridge.

In this transparent cased cartridge, the shot, wad column and powder charge may clearly be seen. This cartridge incorporates the traditional fibre wads.

Cartridge gauges, from left to right: .410, 28-bore, 20-bore, 16-bore, 12-bore, 10-bore, 8-bore, 4-bore.

Because pellets spread more widely the further they go from the muzzle of the gun, and because large pellets retain their energy longer than small ones, the shooter who chooses a cartridge containing a small number of large pellets will find that there is a point at which his pattern becomes too thin to ensure that the target is struck by sufficient pellets to kill it. Although each pellet still retains sufficient energy to inflict vital damage, the chances of a pellet actually striking a vital spot is remote. Sometimes you may hear a shooter boast about a bird which was killed with a single pellet at very great

range. In fact the success of such shots is due to nothing more than luck.

Likewise the shooter who uses a cartridge containing a large number of small pellets will find a point at which, even if the shot is centred upon the target, the pellets have insufficient energy to cause enough shock to kill the quarry. Although the bird or animal may be struck by several pellets, even the combination of all of them will still not be lethal. Individual pellets may, however, cause wounding, and the quarry may fly or run on to die later from its injuries.

No good sportsman will shoot at a quarry which he knows to be out of range for the gun and cartridge he is using. The ability to judge range instinctively and a sure knowledge of the capabilities of one's gun and cartridge are therefore fundamental to good shooting.

Choke

There is, however a device which is fitted to or incorporated within most shotgun barrels, and which regulates the density of the shot pattern independently of range. This is known as 'choke'. A choked barrel is slightly constricted in the last few centimetres before the muzzle. This constriction concentrates or squeezes the shot as it emerges from the barrel and so produces a tighter pattern, which ensures that there is more chance of several pellets striking the target when a shot is taken at longer range. There are five recognised degrees of choke: full choke, three-quarter choke, half choke, quarter choke and improved cylinder. A barrel without any choke at all is said to be true cylinder. A more tightly choked barrel may have a slightly greater effective range than a cylinder barrel, but the shooter must accordingly be more accurate in placing the smaller shot pattern squarely on target.

Most double-barrelled shotguns have one barrel more tightly choked than the other. In a side-by-side shotgun the left barrel is normally choked more tightly than the right, while in an over-and-under shotgun, the top barrel usually has more choke than the bottom one.

Some guns are fitted with a variable choke system, by which a choke tube with the required degree of constriction may be selected and then screwed into the muzzle of the gun, normally with a special key.

If you are at all unsure about which choke to use and which shot size to select, always opt for the more open choke and the smaller shot size, and take only the targets which are well within range. There is no dishonour in not shooting at a bird because you think it may be out of range, and in time you will learn to appreciate and understand the capabilities of your gun.

Cleaning and maintenance

Your gun should be properly looked after. If it is well cared for, regularly maintained and cleaned after use, then a well-built gun may last a lifetime or more. If neglected it will soon deteriorate, lose its value and even become dangerous both to its user and to other people.

Cleaning a gun is a very simple process, which anybody can do immediately after returning from shooting. First the gun should be dismantled by removing the fore-end and detaching the barrels from the action. Immediately wipe off any moisture with an absorbent cloth or a piece of kitchen roll, before getting to work on the barrels. With a mop fitted to the end of your cleaning rod, briskly brush any burnt powder deposit out of the bore. Then remove the mop and brush the bore with a phosphor bronze brush to remove any traces of lead. Finally, using a jag and a cleaning patch with a little gun oil on it, smear the inside of the bore with a thin film of oil. When the barrels are clean inside, wipe them down with an oil-soaked patch, being careful to remove any debris from under the ejectors. Hold the barrels carefully. Sticky fingermarks will leave traces of salt on the metal, and this can in time cause rusting to occur.

A typical shotgun cleaning kit comprising a sectioned cleaning rod, a jag, a phosphor bronze brush and an absorbent mop, gun oil in both liquid and aerosol forms, cleaning patches, and a pair of gunmakers' turnscrews.

Turning next to the action, wipe the metalwork down carefully with an oily patch, taking care to oil beneath the top lever. Do not squirt oil into every hole or aperture, as this will gum up the works when the oil dries and hardens. Nor should you put excessive amounts of oil onto the stock, as this will cause the wood to go soft at the point where it is fitted to the body of the action. However, a small amount of linseed or walnut oil is good for the stock and fore-end, especially after they have become soaked on a wet day.

When shooting in wet weather, it is a good idea to take an absorbent cloth with you in the car to wipe your gun down after shooting. A quick spray over the metalwork with an aerosol gun oil before putting it in its slip will ensure that it has not started to develop rust spots by the time you arrive home. Then, before you start to clean the gun, warm it through by placing it near to a gentle heat source such as a radiator. Alternatively you may play a hair-dryer over it. This will drive off any remaining moisture before you start to clean it.

Although you may in time learn how to carry out simple repairs to your gun, it is far better at first to leave even basic maintenance to the experts. Always remember to take your gun to an experienced gunsmith before the start of the season for an annual overhaul. He will strip the gun down, correct any minor faults and tell you if he thinks that there is anything which requires more serious work. It is far better to get any potential problems put right at this stage than to have a fault develop while you are out shooting, perhaps with disastrous consequences.

VARIABLE CHOKE

When a shotgun barrel is made in the traditional manner, the internal diameter of the bore is often very slightly reduced in the last few centimetres nearest the muzzle in order to provide the 'choke' or constriction which helps to hold the shot pellets closer together in flight, so producing a tighter pattern. Once the gun has been completed, it is possible – though expensive – for a gunsmith to alter the choke. However, because such alteration involves taking away a thin layer of metal from the inside of the bore, choke can only be removed from a gun; never added to it.

Many shooters find that they prefer different degrees of choke for different types of shooting. They may, for example want a tight choke when the targets which they are intending to shoot are likely to be at longer range, and then to switch to a more open choke to shoot at closer range targets without necessarily changing to a different gun. Gunmakers have therefore developed the variable choke system.

There are a number of variants of this system on the market, but all involve the use of carefully engineered choke tubes which may be screwed into the muzzle of the gun. To accommodate these tubes, the inside of the muzzle must first be cut with a screw thread. The shooter will normally have a set of tubes, ranging from open chokes delivering even patterns at short ranges to full or extra-full chokes producing tight patterns for long-range shooting. Choke tubes are fitted to the gun with a special wrench.

Variable choke thus offers flexibility to the shooter who only has one gun but wishes to enjoy a wide range of different types of shooting with it.

Break your gun when putting it into its slip, or when removing it.

Carrying a shotgun over the forearm, with barrels pointing safely at the ground.

Carrying a shotgun safely over the shoulder, trigger guard uppermost, and with barrels pointing skywards.

Holding a shotgun at the ready, when awaiting the chance of a shot.

CHAPTER 3
Gun Safety

There is only one rule which every shooter must unfailingly obey at all times. No matter whether it be in the field, in the home or whilst travelling, the fundamental rule of shooting is gun safety.

Although they may be designed to kill, guns are nothing more than complicated pieces of wood and metal, fixed together in a certain way. They are not in themselves dangerous, for no gun ever shot anyone or anything without outside assistance. There is, therefore, no reason for guns to be feared, but they must always be respected. This respect is the guiding principle behind gun safety. It involves knowing and understanding exactly what a gun is capable of doing, and ensuring that it is only permitted to do it when you, the shooter, want it to.

Handling a shotgun

The shotgun's task is to fire a lethal charge of shot. However, it is not able to do this if it is not loaded, and so the first rule when handling a gun is to check it to see whether or not it contains a cartridge. Whenever you pick up a gun or are passed one by somebody else, the first thing you must do – always and without fail, even if you believe it to be empty – is to open and check it. This reaction must become instinctive and automatic. It takes only a moment to drop down the barrels on a conventional shotgun, or to check the breech and chamber if it is a self-loading or pump-

action one, and it is time well spent. Apart from providing you with the vital information you need as to whether or not the gun is loaded, this will mark you out, when shooting in company, as someone who understands how to handle a gun safely.

When passing a gun to someone else, it must always be unloaded, and it is up to you to demonstrate that this is so by opening it and passing it, stock first, so that the recipient can see the empty breech. If, for whatever reason, you are passed an unopened gun then you must immediately open it and check it. It does not matter if the person who has passed it to you tells you that it is unloaded; check it anyway.

Check your gun when you pick it up, check it before you put it down. Check it when passing it to someone and when receiving it. Check it before putting it in its slip and when you get it out again. Check it before putting it into a vehicle or bringing it into a house, and when you take it out again. Check it before starting to clean it, and before putting it away in its gun cupboard or security cabinet. Whenever you are in doubt as to whether or not your gun is loaded, check it. Even if you are not in doubt, check it. If you do this, at all times and under all circumstances, then you are well on the way to becoming a safe gun handler.

Unless your gun is open, there is no way in which anyone else will be able to determine whether or not it is unloaded. It is therefore up to you to ensure that it is never pointed at anyone or anything that you do not intend to shoot. You must develop what is called 'muzzle awareness'. Always be conscious of where those muzzles are pointing in relation to the people, animals and objects round about you. Ensure that under no circumstances, however fleeting, do they pass across another person.

Even though, having just checked it, you know that your gun is empty, always handle it as though it is loaded. Having a gun pointed at you, however accidentally, is a peculiarly unnerving experience, and the shooter who consistently allows his muzzles to wander where they should not will soon be marked out as someone who is unsafe. He will soon find that he is not welcome to shoot in the company of other people.

Carrying a gun

There has been much debate over the years as to whether a shotgun should, in company, be carried open or closed. Many older shooters were brought up to carry their guns closed, and maintain that to do so places less strain on the action. Even today, you will see some shooters walking or standing around in company with closed guns. Do not copy them. The only way to carry a shotgun when you are with other people is open, unloaded, and held over the crook of the forearm. If you do this, then those standing next to you will be instantly aware that your gun is safe, and they will be put at their ease. On a clay shooting ground, if a person walks around with a closed shotgun which is not securely fastened in a gun slip, then they will be very quickly told to open it, and if they do not do so, they will not find themselves shooting on that ground again.

There is a clear difficulty with self-loading and pump-action shotguns, for however safe the handler may be, it will not always be immediately obvious to a bystander that the gun itself is empty. Some users of self-loading

guns carry with them a cartridge-shaped plug with a coloured ribbon attached. When this is placed in the chamber, with the ribbon hanging out of the loading port, the gun is demonstrated to be empty. Such a device is useful, but even so, the only infallible rule is to ensure that, when carrying a self-loading shotgun in company, the breech is always kept open and the barrel pointed in a safe direction.

Safety in the shooting field

With the principles of gun safety established, let us now look at how a shotgun should be handled in the field. To start with, when you arrive at the place where you will be shooting, be it a farmyard from where you will be departing for a walk along the hedgerows in search of rabbits and pigeons or your numbered peg on a formal driven shoot, you will remove your gun from its slip.

To do so, unbuckle the strap and withdraw the stock of the gun until you reach the top lever. Then, with the barrels still in the slip, open the gun and withdraw it completely with the barrels in the broken position. Likewise, when you are returning your gun to its slip at the end of the drive or after shooting has been completed, do so with the gun broken, closing it only when the barrels are safely within the slip.

Load a shotgun with the barrels pointing at the ground in front of you, with the safety catch engaged in the 'safe' position and with your finger well away from the trigger. Having placed the cartridge or cartridges in the breech, close the gun by bringing the stock up to meet the barrels. This ensures that as the breech snaps shut, the muzzles are still directed at the ground.

Once you have started walking in search of a shot or when you have reached your appointed position and are waiting for your quarry to come past you, you will be doing so with a gun that is both loaded and closed, ready to fire. Therefore the barrels will have to be pointed in a safe direction, and this may be done if you either hold the gun over the crook of your forearm, with the muzzles pointing at the ground, or alternatively if you hold it 'at the ready', with the muzzles pointing up into the air. Both these positions are acceptable when the shooter is either standing or walking. In addition, some shooters find it comfortable when walking-up game, especially over rough ground, to carry the gun over their shoulder, trigger guard upwards, with the barrels pointing safely into the air above them.

You should at all times ensure that the safety catch is engaged until the moment you raise the gun to your shoulder in order to take a shot. A conventional safety catch, mounted on the top strap of the gun, will be safe when it is in the rear position. Normally this will expose an engraved or inlaid 'S'. Try to get into the habit of sliding the safety catch forward as part of the act of mounting the gun rather than disengaging it when you think a shot may shortly present itself. Never, on a formal driven shoot, stand for the entire drive with the safety catch disengaged. Remember that, despite its name, the safety catch does not make the gun safe: only you can do that by unloading it. What the safety catch does is to lock the trigger mechanism. The action meanwhile remains cocked, ready to fire, and it may do so if it receives a jar or blow, even if the safety catch is still on.

If you are using a hammer gun, cock the hammers only when you expect a shot immediately. If that shot is not taken, for whatever reason, then, with the thumb firmly on the hammer and the barrels pointing in a safe direction, carefully pull the trigger and slowly return the hammer to the down position.

Whether you are shooting alone or in company, always be sure before taking a shot, that it is safe to do so. Remember that other shooters, beaters or dogs may be hidden behind trees, bushes or undergrowth. Therefore do not attempt to take a shot

against a backdrop of vegetation that may conceivably hide someone or something you do not intend to shoot. Ideally, you should only shoot at a bird when it is against a clear background of sky, and at an animal such as a rabbit or hare when it is on open ground and you can plainly see everything round about it. However, when in the shooting field ideal conditions rarely occur, and you must learn when it is safe to take a shot and when it is not.

The general rule when shooting at a flying bird, is only to shoot when it is sufficiently high to ensure that your shot cannot strike any person who might be standing close to you, remembering of course that if you are in hilly country there may be people standing well above you whom you cannot see. When shooting at a moving target on the ground, such as a running rabbit, it is all the more important to ensure that your line of fire is absolutely clear, and that there is nothing in the way which might obscure a lurking dog. If you are a guest on an organised shoot, you may sometimes receive the instruction at the beginning to shoot 'no ground game'. Such a rule will have been imposed for safety's sake, to avoid any reason for low shots being taken.

Always ensure that you have a clear view of your quarry before shooting, and that it is not partially hidden by vegetation. Under no circumstances should you shoot through leaves or grass in the hope of hitting something that might be on the other side: you cannot possibly know what else is there.

All this may sound terribly daunting to the beginner, but it is not. In fact it is a simple matter of looking carefully at your surroundings and noting the hazards and unsafe areas around you, then ensuring that if your quarry runs or flies towards those hazards, you do not shoot at it. With practice, you will gradually get used to noting subconsciously where it is safe for you to shoot. Remember that if you have the slightest doubt in your mind, there is absolutely no need for you to pull the trigger. No one will think any the worse of you for holding your fire; indeed, you will be marked out as a thoughtful shot who is conscientious about safety. It is far better not to shoot, even if it is at the only pigeon, pheasant or duck you have seen all day, than to fire an unsafe shot. Once the trigger is pulled, no power on earth can stop the pellets in mid-air and bring them back again.

Crossing obstacles

One of the situations in which shooting acci-dents occur most frequently is when fences, hedges, ditches and other obstacles are being crossed. Very often whilst out shooting you will have to negotiate an obstacle, and there are logical and recognised procedures for doing so which vary according to whether you are alone or in the company of another person.

If you are with somebody else, both of you should open your guns and unload them as you approach the obstacle. Then one of you should pass his gun, broken and unloaded, to the other person and proceed to climb

Crossing a fence alone:

The shooter unloads his gun as he approaches the fence.

He puts down his gun securely on the far side of the fence, so that it will not fall over.

He climbs the fence . . .

. . . picks up his gun . . .

. . . reloads, and continues.

Crossing a fence in company:

Both shooters unload as they approach the fence.

The first shooter passes his gun, open and breech first, to the second and climbs the fence.

His gun is returned, open and breech first.

The first shooter takes the second shooter's gun.

The second shooter climbs the fence.

Both shooters reload their guns and continue.

over the fence, through the hedge or across the ditch. When he gets to the other side and is on firm ground once more, the second shooter should pass both guns, broken and unloaded, to him before crossing the obstacle himself. Then the first shooter should hand back his friend's gun, and the two can continue shooting.

When you are alone, the procedure is different. First unload your gun and pass it through the fence or obstacle, placing it securely on the far side where it will not fall or be damaged. Then climb over or through the obstacle yourself. When you are on the far side, pick up the gun, check it, reload and continue shooting. It might be tempting, when nobody else is about, simply to break your gun and, without removing the cartridges, clamber over a simple obstacle. Do not succumb to this temptation. Many shooters have been found alone, dead or injured, beside a barbed wire fence or thorn hedge which was 'easy' to cross without unloading.

When passing through a gate which simply involves undoing the catch and opening it, it is quite acceptable to break and unload your gun, then carry it through before reloading on the other side. The same goes for foot-bridges, steps and other simple obstacles which do not involve climbing or clambering.

Obstructions in the barrels

Negotiating an obstacle carries with it another risk, that of an obstruction lodging in the barrel. Many shooters are surprised to learn that even a small obstruction such as a twig or a piece of mud or snow can cause severe damage to a gun if it is fired. And if the gun is completely plugged with mud, then discharging it may even cause a burst barrel. After putting your gun down on the ground, and after crossing a muddy ditch or snowy field, always take the trouble to open it and look down the barrels to ensure that they are free from any obstruction.

A rather more serious – and avoidable – cause of obstruction may occur if cartridges of different gauges become mixed. When, for example, a 12-bore user carries both 12- and 20-bore cartridges in the same bag or pocket, it is quite easy, in the heat of the moment, to drop a 20-bore cartridge into the open breech of his gun. Such a cartridge will drop right down into the forcing cone of the chamber, allowing a 12-bore cartridge to be inserted behind it. If this happens and the trigger is pulled, both cartridges will explode together

and so, probably, will the gun. It seems incredible that any shooter can allow such an accident to happen, but sadly it does occur.

Shotguns and vehicles

When travelling in a vehicle to and from the place where you are shooting, you must always unload your gun, and demonstrate to anyone else in the vehicle that it is unloaded, before getting in. Normally you should put your gun back into its slip before getting into a car or other vehicle, as doing so will prevent it being damaged.

A shotgun should never normally be loaded or fired from a vehicle. However, there are certain circumstances in which shooting from a vehicle may take place, such as when rabbits are being shot at night with the aid of a powerful lamp from the back of a pick-up or other four-wheel-drive vehicle. There is nothing wrong with this, provided that safety precautions are rigidly observed. The shooter must have a proper seat, cradle or shooting rest to brace himself against, he must only shoot at quarry which is properly lit and readily identifiable, and he must never shoot over or across the driver or another seated passenger. It is best to keep the number of people in the vehicle down to three at most; a driver, a lamp handler and one shooter. Shooting from a vehicle in this way is a skilled operation, and one which requires consider-able practice. It can be very effective as a means of pest control and very exciting as a form of sporting shooting, but it is not ideally suited to the beginner.

Safety in the home

After shooting you will need to bring your gun into the house to clean it and put it away. On no account should it be loaded indoors, for whatever reason. There is a legal require-ment for guns to be stored securely, but for

When transporting your gun, make sure that it is in its slip or in a secure gun case.

and the importance of maintaining your shotgun in good condition becomes clear.

The ability to recognise a damaged or faulty gun is an important aspect of safe shooting, as is the knowledge of how to prevent such damage from occurring. Common faults include barrels which are dented or bulged as a result of impact damage or excessive internal pressure, perhaps through the gun being fired with an obstruction inside it. Simple bulges and dents are easily rectified by a competent gunsmith, provided that the problem is dealt with promptly.

Another common result of a gun being accidentally dropped or knocked over is a cracked stock. This must be dealt with immediately, and it usually means that the gun must be restocked, that is to say it must have a new stock fitted. If it is not, the crack will become worse and will eventually result in the stock breaking when the gun is fired. Accidental damage can largely be avoided by ensuring that guns are not placed where they can fall over, and by covering them with gun slips when they are not being used. Also, take extra care when there are vehicles about. Insurance companies will confirm that many damaged barrels or broken stocks result from guns being accidentally left on car roofs as the vehicles are driven away or from being left on the ground and driven over.

Poor maintenance may lead to the action of a gun becoming loose over a period of time or to the barrels becoming pitted as a result of corrosion. Both result in a weakening of the gun's structure and in potential danger to the shooter. Other problems can arise through the breaking or malfunction of the internal mechanism. Never use a gun which is malfunctioning; have the fault rectified right away by a professional gunsmith. Always take care to clean your gun after use and to keep it in a state of good mechanical repair. Your local gunsmith will be able to advise you, and to provide an annual overhaul before the start of the shooting season.

safety's sake this should be done anyway. A gun left casually in the home may be picked up by someone who is unfamiliar with guns, possibly an inquisitive child, and it is quite likely that it will be damaged as a result. If there are cartridges near at hand, a terrible accident may occur. Always, therefore, ensure that guns are kept in a locked gun cabinet or some other appropriate form of secure storage, and that cartridges are stored away properly.

Damaged and defective guns

A shotgun is a delicate piece of engineering which is used to create a powerful explosion just a few inches from your face, and thus a faulty or damaged gun can be just as dangerous to the shooter as it is to his intended quarry. Think of it in those terms

Proof

It is a legal requirement that every gun which is sold must bear a recognised proof mark. Such marks are stamped onto the breech end of the barrels and onto the action after the newly manufactured or imported gun has been tested by one of the national proof houses. There are two in Britain – one in London and one in Birmingham. Their job is to test each gun by firing from it, under controlled conditions, a special proof charge which develops many times the internal pressure which the gun would normally experience in the field. After the charge is fired, the gun is thoroughly inspected, and if it passes, then the proof marks will be applied.

However, a gun may become out of proof through wear and tear or by the enlargement and polishing of the barrels to remove pitting. If this is the case it must be submitted for reproof, and it may not be sold until that reproof is passed.

Anyone buying a gun from anywhere other than a recognised gun shop should ensure that a competent firearms dealer first checks it over to ensure that it is in proof and to identify any faults.

Alongside the proof marks on your gun, there will also be stamped an indication of which cartridges it is safe to use. This may give the length of the chamber in inches or millimetres, and as we have already seen, you must not insert into the chamber of a gun a longer cartridge than the one for which it is intended. Alternatively, it may give the maximum service pressure in tons per square inch or kilograms per square centimetre, or perhaps the maximum weight of shot for which the gun is proved. Always check that the information printed on the cartridge box corresponds with that which is stamped on the barrels of your gun.

London	Birmingham	
		Provisional Proof Mark
—		Definitive Proof and View Marks for Black Powder 1813–1904
—	BV BP	Definitive Proof and View Marks for Black Powder 1904–1955
NOT NITRO	BP	Black Powder Proof Mark 1955
NP NITRO PROOF	BP BV NP NITRO PROOF	Definitive Nitro Proof Mark 1904–1955
NP	BNP	Definitive Nitro Proof Mark 1955
	—	Definitive Proof mark (on barrel pre-1955, on action since 1955)
	R	Reproof Mark used since 1925
	SP	Special Proof Mark used since 1925

HEARING PROTECTION

Always wear hearing protection whenever you go shooting.

Regular exposure to loud noises causes progressive damage to the delicate mechanisms of the human ear. Moreover that damage, once it has taken place, is irreversible, and no amount of medical attention can rectify it. The usual result of exposure to noise is a degree of deafness in one or both ears, and sufferers normally experience an inability to hear high frequency sounds. A further effect of noise-induced deafness may be 'tinnitus', in which the sufferer hears a constant high-pitched ringing or whistling noise. Deafness and tinnitus are debilitating. They make it difficult to hear people speaking at normal conversation volume, especially when background noise levels are high.

Shooting exposes participants to repeated high levels of sharp or percussive noise, and everyone who takes part in the sport has a duty to themselves and their families to protect their hearing. Clay pigeon shooters, who may fire very large numbers of cartridges during the course of a competition, have long recognised the need to wear ear protection whilst they are shooting, but the acceptance of hearing protection has only more recently spread to live quarry shooters, which is why many older game shooters today suffer from 'gun deafness'.

Hearing protection comes in two basic forms. Tightly fitting earplugs prevent high frequency noise entering the ear canal, but do not protect the sensitive bones around the outside of the ear. 'Headphone' type ear defenders provide much better all-round protection. In order to overcome the drawback of wearers being unable to hear either their quarry or audible signals such as whistles, some models of ear defenders are fitted with electronic systems which allow through sounds at normal conversational levels, but which filter out loud noises.

Always wear ear protection whenever you go out shooting. If you do not do so, then you will be certain to regret it when your hearing fails as you get older.

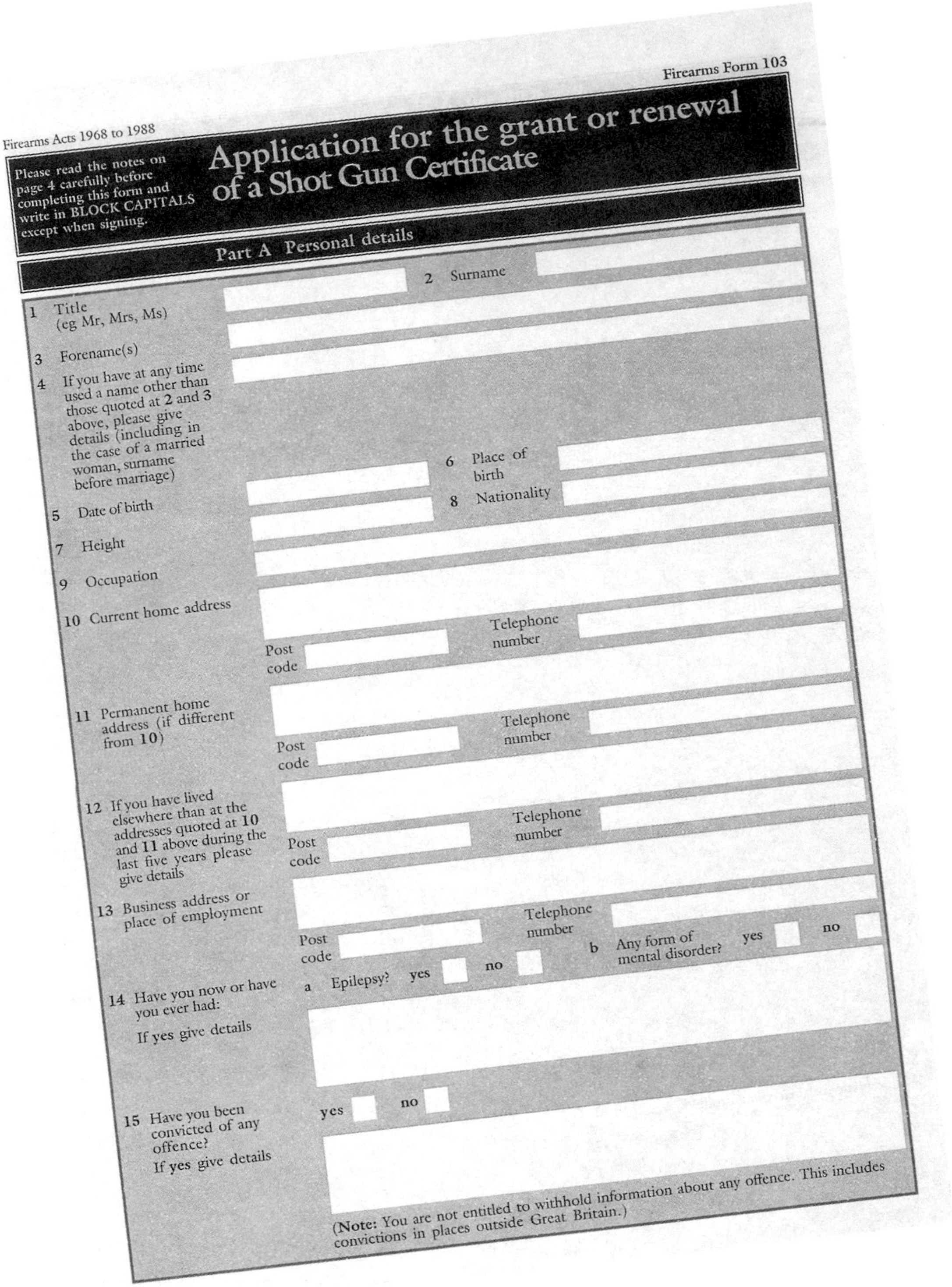

Firearms Form 103

Firearms Acts 1968 to 1988

Please read the notes on page 4 carefully before completing this form and write in BLOCK CAPITALS except when signing.

Application for the grant or renewal of a Shot Gun Certificate

Part A Personal details

1 Title (eg Mr, Mrs, Ms)

2 Surname

3 Forename(s)

4 If you have at any time used a name other than those quoted at 2 and 3 above, please give details (including in the case of a married woman, surname before marriage)

5 Date of birth

6 Place of birth

7 Height

8 Nationality

9 Occupation

10 Current home address

Post code

Telephone number

11 Permanent home address (if different from 10)

Post code

Telephone number

12 If you have lived elsewhere than at the addresses quoted at 10 and 11 above during the last five years please give details

Post code

Telephone number

13 Business address or place of employment

Post code

Telephone number

14 Have you now or have you ever had:

If yes give details

a Epilepsy? yes ☐ no ☐

b Any form of mental disorder? yes ☐ no ☐

15 Have you been convicted of any offence?

If yes give details

yes ☐ no ☐

(**Note:** You are not entitled to withhold information about any offence. This includes convictions in places outside Great Britain.)

Application for a shotgun certificate

CHAPTER 4
Shooting and the Law

The sport of shooting is regulated by a framework of laws which control the possession of guns, define the birds and animals that may be shot and regulate when, where and how it is possible to shoot them. Other laws regulate the sale of game and control poaching. Although it is not necessary for the average shooter to have a complete knowledge of every aspect of shooting law, there are certain things which everyone who shoots must understand.

Shotgun certificates

Firearms, including shotguns and air weapons, are controlled by the Firearms Act 1968 and subsequent amending legislation. These Acts state that in order to possess a shotgun, a person must hold a shotgun certificate. To obtain a certificate, an application must be made to the police force in whose area you normally live. An application form is available from the police, and this must be completed and returned together with the fee payable and four passport-sized photographs of yourself.

The application form must also be countersigned by someone who has known you for at least two years, and who is prepared to say that they know of no good reason why you should not be permitted to possess a shotgun. The regulations state that the person countersigning an application form must be an MP, a magistrate, a minister of religion, a doctor, a lawyer, an established civil servant, a bank officer or a person of similar standing. Since it is accepted that this list may be restrictive and that many applicants for shotgun certificates may not be personally known to people falling into these professional categories, the police allow a degree of flexibility over the selection of countersignatories. One of the photographs submitted with the application form must also be endorsed on the back by the countersignatory to confirm that it is a true likeness of the applicant.

The police will grant a certificate unless the applicant is debarred from possessing firearms by reason of a criminal record or they believe that the applicant might endanger the peace or public safety. There is no need for an applicant to provide good reason for requiring a shotgun, and the law states that sporting and competition shooting and vermin control are sufficient reasons for having a certificate.

A shotgun certificate is valid for five years from the date of grant or renewal, and contains the name, address and photograph of the holder, together with a list of the shotguns he possesses. Also indicated on the certificate is a series of conditions with which the holder must comply. First he must sign it in ink; secondly he must inform the police of the theft or loss of any shotgun to which the certificate relates; thirdly he must inform the police of any change of address; and fourthly the guns must be stored securely.

Most police forces will send an officer to the homes of applicants to check that their storage facilities are indeed secure. However, there is no legal requirement for them to do this. Ultimately it is the duty of the certificate holder to ensure that, so far as is reasonably practicable, he has prevented access to his guns by an unauthorised person. This duty extends both to the home and to the many situations when guns are in use or in transit. There are no regulations concerning the security of guns in parked cars or in other temporary accommodation, but the advice given by the shooting organisations is that they should be kept locked in a car boot or otherwise out of sight in a locked vehicle, with some component such as the fore-end removed so that they are not 'complete'. It is possible to buy devices which clamp or attach the gun to the bodywork of a vehicle, and these may provide additional security and peace of mind.

There is no legal requirement to carry your shotgun certificate when travelling with your gun, but it is strongly advisable to do so whenever you have your gun with you, including while out shooting. You will also have to show it to the retailer each time you wish to buy cartridges.

There are certain rules regarding the transfer of shotguns between certificate holders. Whenever a shotgun is transferred from one person to another, whether it is sold, hired, given or lent, both parties must inform the police within seven days of the transfer, posting their notifications by recorded delivery. The only exceptions are in the case of short-term loans of less than three days, or when the gun is transferred to a registered firearms dealer. The notifications should include the names and addresses of transferor and transferee, plus a full description of the gun in question, including the serial number.

Exemptions

There are a number of exemptions from the need to hold a shotgun certificate.

1   A person such as a loader at a driven game shoot may, without holding a shotgun certificate, have a shotgun and ammunition under instructions from another person, for use by that other person for sporting purposes only.

2   A person may, without holding a shotgun certificate, borrow a shotgun from the occupier of private premises, including land, and use it on those premises in the presence of the occupier. Note that this exemption means just what it says: the gun must have been borrowed from the occupier, the premises must be private, and the occupier must be there when the gun is being used.

3   A person may, without holding a shotgun certificate, use a shotgun at a time and place approved for shooting at artificial targets by the Chief Officer of the police force area within which the place is situated. This allows the use of a gun at recognised shooting schools and clay shoots for which a special authority has been obtained. The exemption only refers to artificial targets, and does not allow live quarry shooting by non-certificate holders.

4   The police may issue a temporary permit to allow a non-certificate holder to possess shotguns. Such a permit, known as a 'Section 7 permit', is normally issued in special circumstances such as where the relative of a deceased person needs time in which to dispose of a shotgun.

5   Temporary visitors to the United Kingdom do not require a shotgun certificate. Instead they need a special

There is no minimum age below which a young person may not hold a shotgun certificate.

visitor's permit, valid for up to 12 months plus, if they are citizens of the European Union, a European Firearms Pass issued by their country of origin. It should be noted that not all EU member states have yet produced these passes.

Shotguns and young people

In law, there is no set age below which persons may not hold a shotgun certificate, and there is no reason why young people of whatever age should not apply for one provided that they are physically capable of handling a gun. Nevertheless, special provi-

sions do apply to the possession and use of shotguns by young people. These are as follows:

1   A person below the age of 15 may not have with him a shotgun unless he is under the direct supervision of a person of 21 or over, or unless the shotgun is in a securely fastened cover so that it cannot be fired. But remember that the young person still requires a shotgun certificate unless covered by one of the exemptions listed on pages 46–47.

2   A person aged between 15 and 17 may be given or lent a shotgun, and may use it without supervision. However, he may not buy or hire a shotgun or ammunition for it.

3   On reaching the age of 17 a person may buy or hire a shotgun and ammunition.

Shooting in public places

Special restrictions apply to the carrying of guns in public places. You may not carry a loaded gun in a public place – that is to say a place to which the public have, or are permitted to have access – without lawful authority or reasonable excuse. Reasonable excuse might include having a loaded shotgun on a footpath running across the land over which you have the right to shoot. In any case, the responsibility for proving lawful authority or reasonable excuse lies with the person carrying the gun.

Particular care must be taken when you are shooting close to public roads. It is an offence under the Highways Act 1980 to discharge any firearm within 50 ft (15 m) of the centre of a highway without lawful authority or reasonable excuse if in consequence someone using the highway is injured, interrupted or endangered.

Armed trespass

Whenever you are shooting, you must make absolutely certain that you have authority to be where you are. If you have no such authority, and have a gun with you, whether it is loaded or not, then you are committing an armed trespass. While normally trespass is a civil offence, armed trespass is a criminal matter and carries with it a severe penalty. It is therefore wise to leave your gun behind if you need to enter land over which you do not have the shooting rights, for example to retrieve a bird which has fallen beyond your boundary.

Sporting rights and poaching

Unlike some other European countries, which have large areas of land in which local people may shoot freely, Britain has for a very long time maintained strict controls over the enjoyment of shooting or sporting rights in the countryside. Under these controls, the rights to shoot on any particular piece of land are almost always privately owned, and the owner is usually, though not always, also the landowner. Although this may sound very restrictive, in practice it has meant that game birds and many other wild species have remained far more abundant in Britain than elsewhere. The reason is that because a landowner or holder of sporting rights knows that he alone controls the shooting over a piece of land, he has the incentive to preserve and protect the game there in the knowledge that someone else is not able simply to walk in and shoot it.

This does, of course, mean that you must be very careful to ensure that before you go shooting you have the permission of the landowner or the holder of the sporting rights. If you do not, then you will be poaching and very likely committing an armed trespass into the bargain. Poaching may be dealt with severely by the courts, and night poaching is a particularly serious offence.

Shooting wild birds

The law relating to the shooting of wild birds, as distinct from game, is covered by the Wildlife and Countryside Act 1981. This Act prescribes lists of birds which may be shot under certain circumstances and prohibits some methods of killing or taking birds.

The prohibited methods are as follows:

1 using a semi-automatic weapon which is capable of holding more than two rounds in the magazine

2 using a shotgun of which the internal diameter at the muzzle exceeds 1¾ inches

3 using any device for illuminating a target or any sighting device for night shooting

4 using any form of artificial light or any mirror or other dazzling device

5 using as a decoy any sound recording

6 using any mechanically propelled vehicle, including a boat, in immediate pursuit of a wild bird for the purpose of killing it

Furthermore, it is not permissible to use as a decoy any live bird which is tethered, secured, blind, maimed or injured.

Under the Wildlife and Countryside Act 1981, the following wild birds may be killed or taken by authorised persons during the open season:

Coot
Gadwall
Goldeneye
Golden plover
Goose, Canada
Goose, greylag
Goose, pink-footed
Goose, white-fronted (in England and Wales only)
Mallard
Moorhen
Pintail
Pochard
Shoveler
Snipe, common
Teal
Tufted duck
Wigeon
Woodcock

Seasons for wild birds

The seasons within which wild birds may be taken are as follows:

Woodcock (England and Wales)
                    1 October – 31 January
Woodcock (Scotland)
                    1 September – 31 January
Snipe   12 August – 31 January
Wild duck and geese (inland)
                    1 September – 31 January
Wild duck and geese (below the high
  water mark of ordinary spring tides)
                    1 September – 20 February
Coot, moorhen, golden plover
                    1 September – 31 January

It is illegal to shoot these species on Christmas Day in England, Scotland and Wales, and on Sundays in Scotland and in the following English and Welsh counties (or former counties) and county boroughs: Anglesey, Brecknock, Caernarfon, Cardigan, Carmarthen, Cornwall, Denbigh, Devon, Doncaster, Glamorgan, Great Yarmouth County Borough, Isle of Ely, Leeds County Borough, Merioneth, Norfolk, Pembroke, Somerset and the North and West Ridings of Yorkshire.

In Northern Ireland there is no shooting on the foreshore after 31 January and all wild birds are protected at night and on Sundays. Duck and goose species which may be shot are gadwall, goldeneye, mallard, pintail, pochard, scaup, shoveler, teal, tufted duck, wigeon, greylag goose, pink-footed goose, Canada goose. Waders which may be shot are common snipe, curlew, golden plover, jack snipe, woodcock.

Severe weather

The Secretary of State for the Environment may declare periods of special protection for wild birds, during which the shooting of wild-fowl, snipe and woodcock is prohibited. These are normally declared as a result of severe weather conditions, and a strict set of criteria has been agreed by the Government, the shooting organisations and the bird protection bodies for approving and implementing them.

Pest species

Certain other species of wild birds may be killed or taken by authorised persons at all times, under annual open and general licences issued by the Department of the Environment. This means that individuals do not have to apply for a licence. These are often described as 'pest' species and are usually shot to prevent serious damage to agriculture or for the conservation of wild birds. They are:

Collared dove
Crow
Gull, greater black-backed
Gull, lesser black-backed
Gull, herring
House sparrow
Jackdaw
Jay
Magpie
Pigeon, feral
Rook
Starling
Woodpigeon

Shooting game

The law relating to the killing or taking of game is enshrined in a series of Acts of Parliament, the most important of which is the Game Act 1831. Not surprisingly, this piece of legislation appears very old fashioned in places, but it nevertheless remains on the statute book, and therefore provides the legal framework within which all game shooting

takes place. The Game Act lists the species which are normally referred to as game: black grouse, pheasant, partridge, red grouse, ptarmigan and hares.

Seasons for game

The seasons within which game may be taken are as follows:

Black grouse	20 August – 10 December
Pheasant	1 October – 1 February
Partridge	1 September – 1 February
Red grouse and ptarmigan	
	12 August – 10 December
Hares	No close season

Although there is no close season for hares, they may not be offered for sale between 1 March and 31 July. With the exception of hares, game may not be shot at night, i.e. from one hour after sunset to one hour before sunrise, nor on Sundays or Christmas Day.

Shooting rabbits and hares

The Ground Game Act 1880 gives every occupier of land the right to kill and take rabbits and hares. The original intention of this law was to ensure that tenant farmers had the right to protect their crops from damage.

Rabbits and hares may be shot at night by the landowner or by persons authorised by him. An occupier of land, together with one other person authorised by him, may also shoot rabbits and hares at night provided that he has the permission of the holder of the sporting rights if he does not hold them himself.

The sale of dead game and wild birds

At the end of a day's shooting, game is often sold in order to defray the costs of running the shoot. However, it may only be sold to a game dealer licensed by the local authority. The dealer, who has to meet strict regulations concerning the hygiene of his premises, may then sell it to the public. To sell game other than to a licensed dealer is illegal unless you yourself are also a licensed dealer.

Game may only be sold dead during the open season, and for a period of ten days after the season closes. Special provisions exist regarding the sale of hares, which have no close season. Rabbits and pigeons, which have no close season, may be sold dead at any time of the year.

Certain other wild birds may be sold dead between 1 September and 28 February:

Coot
Golden plover
Mallard
Pintail
Pochard
Shoveler
Snipe, common
Teal
Tufted duck
Wigeon
Woodcock

It is illegal to sell dead wild geese.

The protection of wild animals

The law provides protection for wild animals, and lists certain species which are specially protected. None of these is likely to be encountered by most shooters, with the possible exception of the red squirrel. Certain methods of killing or taking wild animals are prohibited, including using a self-locking snare, a bow or crossbow or any explosive other than ammunition for a firearm or shotgun, and using a live mammal or bird as a decoy.

Game Licence

A game licence is required to shoot black game, grouse, hare, partridge, pheasant, ptarmigan, snipe and woodcock. Game licences may be purchased from the larger post offices and are available to cover any of the following periods:
Annually expiring 31 July
1 August to 31 October
1 November to 31 July
Any period of 14 days

Non-Toxic shot

The use of lead shot in England and Wales is prohibited:

On or over any area below the high water mark of ordinary spring tides

On or over particular Sites of Special Scientific Interest (SSSI) which are important for waterfowl

For the shooting of any duck, goose, moorhen or coot

A prohibition on the use of lead is therefore in place for all shooting over certain wetland areas, whether it be for wildfowl, game or pest species. In addition, the species named within the legislation may not be shot using lead cartridges in any circumstances, even on a driven game shoot over farmland. Game shoots on which ducks are shot and those operating over listed SSSIs must ensure that non-toxic shot is used where appropriate.

The legislation applies only to shotgun shooting. It remains legal, for example, to control pests over a wetland SSSI using lead bullets or slugs from a rifle.

Driven game shooting became very fashionable during the Edwardian period.

CHAPTER 5
Game Shooting

A combination of factors led to the establishment of driven game shooting in Britain in the nineteenth century. The development of the breech-loading shotgun meant that sportsmen no longer had to load their guns laboriously from the muzzle after each shot, and were able to increase their rate of fire greatly. This meant that they could successfully shoot at a steady stream of birds driven over them by a team of assistants. At the same time, the wealth created by the Industrial Revolution enabled landowners to engage vast teams of staff to help on large organised shoots. Finally, the system of land ownership which existed in Britain meant that game could be preserved for shooting over the entire area of large estates. Landowners started to invest large sums of money in redesigning their estates to accommodate woods and spinneys which would improve the habitat for game and game shooting. The result was the creation of the great driven game shoots which had their high-water mark in the Edwardian period before the First World War.

What is game shooting?

A driven game shoot simply means one in which the shooters, or 'guns', instead of flushing the birds themselves and shooting them as they fly away, wait at prearranged stands, or 'pegs', while a team of beaters drives the game towards them. If it is well organised, a driven shoot will deliver birds which are flying high and fast, and which therefore test shooting skills to the extreme.

On the majority of driven shoots, the pheasant is by far the most important quarry species. A native of the Middle East, this bird was introduced to Britain some 2,000 years ago. It is strong and flies very fast over short distances, it adapts well to a variety of habitats and it can easily be reared and introduced to the wild. This is important, as driven game shooting requires a plentiful population of game if it is to be successful. Although some shoots in areas of particularly favourable habitat can rely on wild pheasants to form the bulk of their bag, many more need to augment the wild stock by rearing and releasing birds.

The rearing and releasing of game, the management of the birds and their habitat and the control of predators is the responsibility of the gamekeeper. Many estates and shoots employ full-time gamekeepers; others work part-time or as amateurs. On the day of a shoot, it is the responsibility of the gamekeeper to marshal and direct the other assistants, whose job it is to ensure that the birds are flushed and directed over the guns to present challenging, sporting shots. These assistants include the beaters, who walk in line through the cover in order to move the birds forwards and flush them over the guns; the stops, who are positioned at strategic points to prevent birds escaping out of the cover without flying over the guns; and the

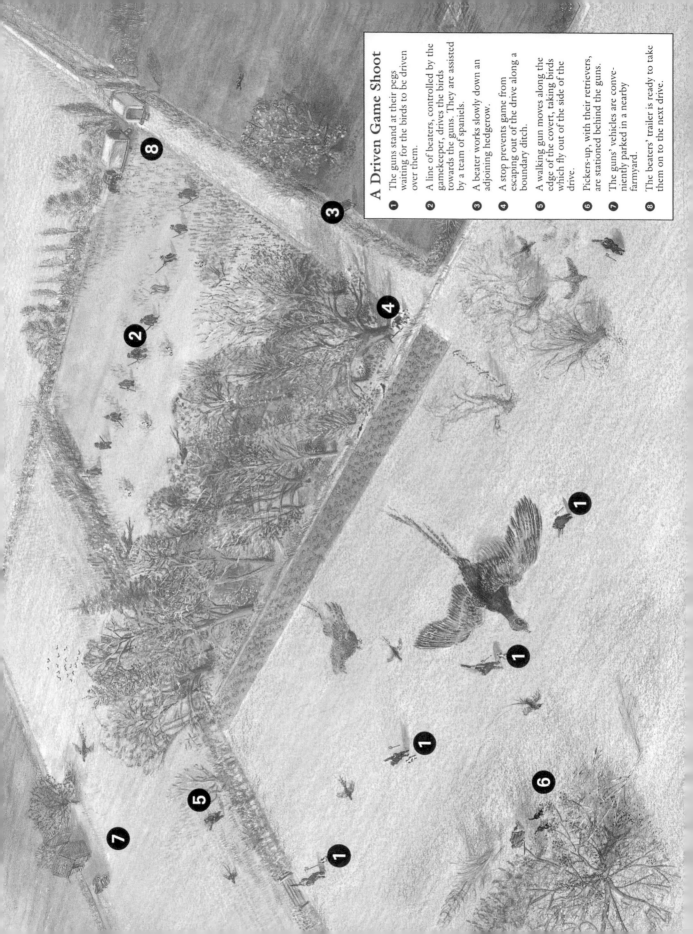

A Driven Game Shoot

1 The guns stand at their pegs waiting for the birds to be driven over them.

2 A line of beaters, controlled by the gamekeeper, drives the birds towards the guns. They are assisted by a team of spaniels.

3 A beater works slowly down an adjoining hedgerow.

4 A stop prevents game from escaping out of the drive along a boundary ditch.

5 A walking gun moves along the edge of the covert, taking birds which fly out of the side of the drive.

6 Pickers-up, with their retrievers, are stationed behind the guns.

7 The guns' vehicles are conveniently parked in a nearby farmyard.

8 The beaters' trailer is ready to take them on to the next drive.

pickers-up, who work their dogs behind the line of guns in order to retrieve the shot game.

Shoots vary greatly in size. At one end of the scale are the very grand traditional estate shoots, in which many helpers are employed to make sure the day runs smoothly and at which guests often stand with the guns to watch the shooting. Sometimes the guns use pairs of shotguns and have loaders, whose task it is to load the second shotgun while the first is in use. Shoots like this are important social occasions and normally a lunch is laid on for the guns and their guests. Shooting on this scale is expensive, and the large shoots often let several days during the season to paying guns in order to recover a proportion of the costs involved. Some shoots are run on entirely commercial lines to return a profit to the estate.

Far more frequent are the modest shoots in which a group or 'syndicate' of guns club together in order to fund the cost of rearing and releasing the birds. The farmer or landowner over whose land the shoot operates may be a member of the syndicate, and very frequently the guns themselves carry out the work involved in game management. A syndicate member who lives close to the shoot may act as amateur gamekeeper and ensure that the birds are fed and watered, and that predators are kept under control.

Many shooters get their first taste of driven game shooting when they receive an invitation to attend a shoot as a guest of one of the regular guns. Others may buy a day at one of the commercial shoots. In either case, a first day at driven game is usually both exciting and daunting. There is so much to think about, and a great deal of preparation to be done, even before the day itself arrives.

TOP RIGHT:
The side-by-side double-barrelled shotgun is very popular amongst game shooters.

Your gun should be returned securely to its slip between drives.

A day's driven pheasant shooting

Whether it is an expensive shoot or a modest one, the first thing you must do upon receiving an invitation to a driven game shoot is to reply promptly. The shoot organiser will be putting a great deal of effort into making the day a success, and he will want to know at the outset that he has a full team of guns.

Shoot days are planned weeks or even months in advance, so there is normally plenty of time to anticipate the big day and to think about what clothing and equipment you are going to take with you. First on the list will be your gun. A conventional double-barrelled shotgun is most appropriate, and it does not matter whether it is of the traditional side-by-side or the over-and-under configuration. It is best to avoid pump-action and semi-automatic weapons since, as we have already seen, they cannot always immediately be seen to be safely unloaded when you are shooting in the company of other people. Most game shooters use a 12-bore gun, although many experienced shots today prefer the 20-bore, and the 20 is frequently the choice of women shooters and young shots. A gun slip will be necessary to cover your gun between drives.

Select the correct cartridges to go with your gun. A standard game load of between 28 g (1 oz) and 32 g (1^1/$_8$ oz) will be suitable (for 12-bore guns), and shot size 6 or 7 will be best if you are expecting to encounter pheasants or partridges. Some shoots prefer you to use fibre-wadded cartridges to prevent the problem of litter caused by plastic monowads, and although you will of course try to pick up all your empty cartridges, paper cases are still popular in the game shooting field because if a few empties are not recovered, they are at least biodegradable. You must also assess how many cartridges to take with you. Check with your host: he will normally give you guidance on this point. But remember that it is better to have too many than too few. You can always bring them home again with you, but to run out of cartridges in the middle of a drive is the height of frustration.

Although a cartridge belt is an easy way of carrying your ammunition, most only hold 25 rounds, and on a driven day you can often expect to fire more cartridges than that, so a cartridge bag is a better option for the game shooter, especially as he will normally be standing at a fixed point while he is shooting and so will not have to carry his cartridge bag and shoot at the same time. Cartridge bags can be obtained with a variety of capacities. It is also possible to obtain a traditional cartridge magazine which will carry several hundred cartridges. Left in the car, this will ensure a 'strategic reserve' of ammunition.

Although working their own gundogs is very important to many shooters, driven game shooting is the branch of the sport in which a dog is of least significance, as there are normally experienced pickers-up in attendance to ensure that all the game is retrieved. Indeed, some larger shoots actively discourage guns from bringing their own dogs. The smaller ones, however, are more likely to welcome guns' dogs. In any case, check with your host before bringing a dog to a driven shoot. On your first few days of game shooting you would be well advised to leave the dog behind. It will only be an extra worry on your mind during a day when you will want to focus all your concentration on your shooting. As you gain experience in the field, then by all means take your dog if the shoot organiser is happy with your doing so. Only do so if it is well trained, however, and if there is the slightest risk of it being unsteady and of wanting to run-in to falling game or the sound of gunshots, do not be embarassed to make sure that it is firmly secured by a slip lead and a dog anchor.

Because of the social nature of game shooting, a great deal of attention has always been given to the correct form of dress. Although it is important to be properly turned out, out of courtesy both to your host and the other guns and to ensure your own peace of mind, codes of dress for game shooting attract far more attention than they actually deserve. At all but the very smartest shoots, a pair of breeks or plus-twos worn with woollen stockings and boots or wellingtons, and a waxproofed jacket over a comfortable sweater are more than adequate. With a collar and tie and a tweed or waxproof hat, you are there. Upgrade the waxproof to a tweed field coat and you are dressed well enough for the smartest occasion.

On the day of the shoot, make sure that you arrive in good time. You will be greeted by your host and the shoot captain, who will provide you and the other guns with a briefing on the rules of the shoot. He will stress the importance of safe shooting, and will tell you whether or not the shooting of ground game, that is to say rabbits and hares, is permitted. Some shoots prefer the guns not to shoot ground game, especially close to woodland, in case a stray shot injures someone. Other shoots prefer to preserve hares. Most gamekeepers will be only too delighted for you to shoot a fox if you get the chance, but do not attempt to do so unless you are very close indeed, for a shotgun loaded with bird shot is not really the most suitable weapon for foxes. And if you are in foxhunting country and your host welcomes the hounds on his land, then it is best to leave foxes altogether.

The shoot captain will also explain any signals given to start and finish the drives. These are normally given on a horn or a whistle. Unless you are given instructions to the contrary, you must not load your gun until you hear the signal to start the drive, and you must unload as soon as you hear the signal that it is over.

You will then be invited to draw for your place, normally by selecting a numbered tab. The number you draw will give you the number of the peg at which you will stand for the first drive. It is usual for the guns to move up two places between drives, so that the gun who is at number 4 for the first drive becomes number 6 on the second and so on. This ensures that no one unfairly monopolises the best of the shooting all day. At most shoots the drives will be pegged for between eight and ten guns.

At this point, you and your fellow guns will move off, either on foot or aboard a vehicle, and you will be directed to your peg for the first drive. Let us imagine that it is a fine, crisp November morning, and your numbered peg is situated in the bottom of a shallow valley, where the grass is still white from the night's frost. In front of you is a dark covert, and behind is more woodland. To the left and right, you see your fellow guns, getting themselves ready to shoot. The first thing you will do is to remove your cartridge bag and anything else that you are carrying, and to place them on the ground in front of you. It is a good idea to put a sufficient quantity of cartridges in your pockets so that you can reload quickly without constantly having to reach down during the drive. Remove your gun, broken, from its slip, check the barrels for obstructions, and do not load until you hear the signal that the drive is about to start.

Now is the time to take your bearings. Check behind you to see if there are any pickers-up that you should be aware of. Similarly, look out for stops in the wood ahead, and make a mental note of your safe zones of fire. High birds coming over you or crossing in front of you may be shot at. You may also shoot at birds behind the line of guns if it is safe to do so, remembering of course that if you wish to turn and take a shot behind then you must first dismount the gun from your shoulder, with the barrels pointed directly upwards, remounting it only when you are facing a safe firing zone. Any low birds should be left: they only encourage dangerous shooting. You should also leave any bird which you can see will make a better driven shot for your neighbouring gun than it will for you. It is galling to raise your gun at

a high pheasant coming directly at you, only to see it crumple and fall at your feet from your neighbour's shot: nobody likes to stand next to a 'poacher', as a greedy shooter is sometimes called.

The whistle blows, and you slip two cartridges into the breech and close your gun. Far away, at the distant end of the covert, the beaters are starting to move, tapping with their sticks to nudge the pheasants forward. It is some minutes before the birds start flushing, a time of tension as you stand alert, waiting, watching, listening. Then, further down the line there is the whirr of wings and the crowing of a cock pheasant as the first bird soars high over the guns. A spatter of shots and it sails serenely on, to be lost in the woods behind. Then a flush of birds, this time directly in front of you. Your neighbour takes one cleanly on your left, while a second bird seems to come directly for the gap between the two of you. Is it your bird or his? In the moment that it takes you to decide to shoot, the bird, a fine cock pheasant in full autumn plumage, has accelerated through the gap and your shot is yards behind its tail. You turn to see that, while you have been engaged with the cock on your left, a sneaky hen has come

straight over your head. You miss that too. Such is driven game shooting.

All is not lost, however. You reload quickly to see another cock heading towards you. This time the gun is mounted smoothly, the swing is sweet and the shot sure. Your first driven pheasant tumbles to the ground 10 metres behind you.

All too quickly you hear the whistle which signals that it is time to unload. By now the beaters can be seen coming through the last few metres of cover, and the drive is at an end. As you return your gun safely to its slip, you turn to see the pickers-up, stationed well back from the line of guns, busy with their dogs collecting the shot game. Perhaps one of them approaches you to congratulate you on your shooting and to establish that all your birds have been retrieved. Then, with the memory of that first driven pheasant still fresh in your mind, and with a feeling of elation, you turn to join the other guns and share with them success and failure as you move on to the next drive.

High driven birds will test your shooting skill.

The end of a drive, and a chance to compare notes with the other guns.

The last drive of the day. An opportunity to reflect on the day's sport.

On many organised driven shoots, lunch is arranged after the third or fourth drive. It can be anything from a formal affair indoors to a relaxing break in a barn, where the guns and beaters recall the morning's events. You should make sure that you have checked with your host regarding the lunch arrangements, and established whether or not you are expected to bring your own food and vacuum flask. You may also be invited to have a drink with the other guns, either at lunch-time or between drives. If you do so, then please take care. Alcohol and guns can be a dangerous mixture, and drink is the cause of many a rash or risky shot.

There is one other important point which must be checked with your host. On a formal shoot where a gamekeeper is employed, it is traditional to offer him a tip at the end of the day, in appreciation of the sport which has resulted from his hard work throughout the year. Tipping can sometimes be a sensitive point, so it is best to enquire discreetly of your host beforehand whether or not it is required, and if so how much is appropriate. The correct time to quietly offer the keeper his tip, together with a word of thanks for the day, is when he hands you the traditional brace of birds to take home with you.

Partridges

So far we have looked only at driven pheasant shooting. On many of the more open estates and farms, often in the drier counties of the south and east of England, partridges are the main quarry in the early part of the shooting season. Although there are some wild partridge shoots, where the traditional gamekeeping skills of predator control and habitat management ensure that, in a good year, a shootable surplus of wild partridges is present, most partridge shoots today rear and release birds. You will encounter two species of partridge on shoots in Britain, the native grey partridge and the introduced red-legged or French partridge, which is particularly well suited to rearing and releasing. Because the partridge shooting season opens a month before that for pheasants, many shoots which have both partridges and pheasants organise a few days of partridge shooting before turning to the main pheasant coverts later in the year.

Partridges provide extremely fast, testing targets, often coming through the line in 'coveys' or groups of birds a dozen or more strong. This makes them particularly challenging targets for the guns, because it is all too easy, when faced with a fast-flying covey sweeping towards you like a swarm of bees, to dither over which bird you are going to shoot at. In that moment of hesitation, the chance of a successful shot will vanish. The skilled partridge shooter therefore instantly picks his bird as the covey approaches and takes his shot as early as possible before perhaps turning to take a second bird behind. The degree of skill involved ensures that partridge shooting is highly prized by experienced game shooters.

Partridges are birds of arable farmland, and they thrive where there is a mix of different crops, such as cereals and root crops, growing in close proximity. Traditionally, they were shot over the stubble fields left after harvest in early autumn, but for many years the dominance of autumn-sown cereals has meant that the stubbles have been ploughed as soon as harvest is completed. Now, however, the European Union's set-aside scheme, designed to reduce the area of land planted with cereals, has meant that farmers are able to leave their autumn stubbles for much longer again, and this has greatly benefited partridges, as well as a host of other wild birds.

Nevertheless, where partridges are released, cover is required to provide them with food, shelter and protection. This is often planted by farmers and landowners in the form of strips or blocks of maize, kale or other cover crops grown specifically for game management. Very often, these cover crops will be walked through by the beaters in order to drive partridges over the guns.

Grouse

Partridges and pheasants are the main species of game bird which you are likely to encounter on a conventional lowland shoot. There is, however, a very different form of game shooting on the heather moors of Scotland, northern England and a few parts of Wales. Grouse shooting is reckoned by many shooters to be the finest of all forms of game shooting. Not only is the red grouse an exceptionally fast and agile bird, offering some of the most difficult of all shooting, but it also has its home in the most glorious upland countryside. Once experienced, the combination of sporting shooting and magnificent scenery is never forgotten, and draws grouse shooters back to the moors year after year.

The red grouse is unique to the British Isles, and since it cannot be commercially reared, grouse shooting relies entirely on the creation of a suitable habitat in which the birds can breed and flourish, and on the control of predators such as foxes. This time-consuming and laborious habitat management and predator control work is the job of the moorland gamekeeper.

Driven grouse shooting

Where the moor is actively managed to ensure a high population of grouse, driven shooting is normally practised. As in driven pheasant shooting, teams of beaters are employed to drive the coveys towards the guns. There, however, the similarity ends. Grouse drives take place across wide, open moorland, and the beaters often have to walk many miles in order to move the coveys forward and ensure that they end up flying over the guns. Their job is an arduous one, especially when

Driven grouse shooting. This Lancashire grouse butt has been beautifully built of turf and stone.

the weather is very hot or when the rain lashes down later in the year.

Unlike in pheasant shooting, where the guns are generally positioned in the open, grouse shooters are normally concealed in specially constructed butts. These may either be temporary screens made of wood and wire mesh or permanent, circular structures, often beautifully built of turf and stone. Because of the length of time it can take the beaters to drive the grouse towards them, grouse shooters are often thankful for the shelter which a well-built butt provides.

If you are lucky enough to be invited to shoot driven grouse, there are a number of additional points which you should bear in mind. Grouse travel very fast indeed when they are flying towards you in a drive. But they also fly very low, hugging the contours of the ground like surface-skimming missiles, and they can be upon you before you have time to think. Rather like partridges, they frequently cross the line of butts in coveys and later in the autumn these coveys often amalgamate into large packs. It is therefore essential that you select your bird well in

Grouse provide some of the most exciting game shooting in Britain.

front and shoot early. If you leave a driven grouse too long before shooting, it will almost certainly have crossed the butts and be out of range before you have had time to bring your gun to bear.

The sheer speed and agility of the grouse makes driven grouse shooting very exciting indeed, although the periods of excitement may be interspersed with long spells of waiting while the beaters bring the drive in towards the butts. Excitement, however, can lead to lapses in safety. Always remember that you may only take birds which are in front, behind or well up above your butt. Never on any account shoot down the line of the butts at a low-flying target, for in doing so you may

easily cause serious injury to someone. Butts are often fitted with short sticks placed around their edges to mark the angles within which it is safe to shoot.

Try to mark down any grouse you shoot. There will probably be pickers-up stationed well back to collect any birds which fall behind the line, but when the drive is over, the dogs will need to retrieve the grouse which have dropped close to the butts, and your guidance here will prove invaluable, for even if a bird is no more than 20 or 30 metres away, it is surprising how difficult it can be to find if it falls in deep heather.

Walked-up grouse

On moors where there are not sufficient grouse to justify the very considerable cost of driven shooting, grouse are more usually walked-up. This is a less formal and far more energetic form of sport, in which the guns themselves, often with a few non-shooting friends, walk in line across the moor in an effort to flush grouse from the heather in front of them and shoot the birds as they fly off. Walking perhaps many miles across a grouse moor, particularly in August or early September, is hard work, but the rewards are enormous. Not only do you experience all the excitement of grouse shooting, but you also get the chance to see a wonderful heather-clad landscape as it unfolds around you, and perhaps also to watch the dogs working as they hunt back and forth after the elusive coveys.

Grouse shooter and English pointer. Shooting over pointing dogs is one of the oldest forms of grouse shooting.

When walking-up grouse, make sure you keep in line.

Dress for walked-up grouse shooting is much more casual than for the formality of a driven day. The most important element is a good pair of stout ankle boots which will keep your feet comfortable all day over rough terrain. On a warm August day, all that may be required for your top half is a shooting vest over a short-sleeved shirt, but a sweater or jacket may be more sensible if the weather is cooler. Remember that the temperature is likely to be lower when you are high up on the moor, and remember also that anything you need during the day, whether it be waterproof clothing, food or spare cartridges, may well have to be carried with you if it cannot be left at some strategic point in a vehicle. It is too late, when you are 600 metres up a Scottish mountain and it is coming on to rain, to decide that you need that waterproof coat you left back at base.

When walking-up grouse, make sure that you stay in line and follow the instructions of the keeper or shoot captain. In rough country it is sometimes very easy to lose touch with the guns or walkers on either side of you, so make sure you are aware at all times where it is safe to shoot. On steep slopes, the person next to you may be several metres higher than you are, so take extra care when shooting at birds which fly through the line. A shot which, if taken on flat ground would be at an elevation which is perfectly safe, when translated onto a steeply sloping grouse moor might well endanger a gun or walker above you in the line.

On a walked-up day, you are effectively combing each section of the moor in turn and hoping to flush whatever birds are there, perhaps with the aid of close-hunting dogs like spaniels. There is, however, a third method of shooting grouse in which a pointing dog is used to find the birds and so allow one or two guns to get into position for a shot before they are flushed. Dogging the moors with pointers or setters is the oldest form of grouse shooting and is a very specialised form of sport. A pointing dog is used to quarter over the moor in an attempt to catch the scent of a hidden covey. It may range a long way in front of the guns, but when it scents birds ahead it halts and stands rigidly, 'pointing' at them. The guns then hurry forward to where it is standing, upon which the handler allows his dog to flush the grouse, hopefully giving the guns the chance of a shot. If the pointer is not trained to retrieve, then a specialist retriever will be used to pick up the fallen grouse. If you enjoy watching traditional working dogs going about the task for which they have been bred and trained, then you should never turn down the opportunity of a day's dogging for grouse.

Other grouse species

From the shooter's point of view, the red grouse is by far the most important of the grouse species to be found in the British Isles. There are, however, three other related species which are occasionally encountered.

The black grouse is found on the moorland edges, often amongst scattered groups of birch or rowan trees. It is larger than the red grouse and its strong, fast flight is less aerobatic. Black grouse were once found on moors and heaths all over southern England, but they are today in serious decline, probably because of changes in habitat, and are now to be found only in the uplands.

Ptarmigan are birds of the tundra, and are the only British species of grouse to change colour with the seasons, turning white as winter approaches to match the snowy landscape of their natural habitat. They live on rocky mountain tops in the Scottish highlands, normally at altitudes in excess of 800 metres. Ptarmigan shooting is a specialised form of sport which involves a great deal of arduous climbing.

Capercaillie, though once native to Britain, became extinct here and had to be reintroduced from Scandinavia. Their natural habitat is the old Caledonian pine forest of the Scottish highlands, where they live on a diet of pine needles. They are large birds, the size of a small turkey, and are unmistakable as they crash through the branches of the pine wood. However, like the Caledonian forest itself they are becoming increasingly rare, and the capercaillie is now protected by law.

Ptarmigan

Black Grouse

GAME BIRDS

The Pheasant

Nobody can possibly mistake the pheasant for any other bird. The gaudy cock pheasant, with its speckled bronze body and wings, its iridescent green head and neck, its long tail and scarlet cheek patches, is one of the most striking of all birds in the British countryside. Its mate is smaller in size and considerably more dowdy, being a uniform brown in colour.

Pheasants are indigenous to central and south Asia, and are only present in Europe as a result of deliberate introduction by man. It is generally believed that the species was brought to Britain by the Romans, and pheasant remains have been found in excavations dating from the period. The first record of pheasants dates from Norman times, and it was probably then that the first large-scale

introductions took place. Today pheasants are found widely throughout Great Britain, and are absent only from the Scottish highlands and the Welsh mountains.

Mixed farmland interspersed with woodland is the pheasant's preferred habitat, and birds particularly enjoy woods with thick undergrowth to provide them with warmth and shelter. They nest on the ground, laying from 7 to 18 eggs, normally between late April and June. Rearing and releasing of pheasants for shooting takes place widely throughout the country, and there has been regular interbreeding between wild and reared populations.

The Grey Partridge

The grey or 'English' partridge is a bird of traditional mixed open farmland, and one which has suffered considerably from the intensification of farming over the past forty years. As a result, numbers are in general

decline, although the grey partridge is still present throughout lowland Britain.

Small and dumpy in appearance, with grey upper plumage and a distinctive horseshoe-shaped chestnut marking on the breast, grey partridges remain together in family groups or coveys well into the winter. In January or February they pair up and in spring clutches of 10–20 eggs are laid in a shallow and well camouflaged depression, normally beneath or beside a hedgerow. Hatching of the chicks occurs in early June, coinciding with the peak availability of the insect food on which the young birds rely. In the wild, chicks only switch to eating seeds and grains as they get older, and a ready availability of insect grubs is thus essential to their survival in the first few days of life. As a result, the widespread use of farm pesticides is particularly damaging to wild partridge populations.

The grey partridge is a strong and powerful flyer over short distances, and its ability to turn and climb rapidly as it bursts over a hedgerow earned it a reputation as one of our premier sporting birds. Where rearing and releasing occurs, grey partridges are regularly shot. Organised wild grey partridge shooting, however, only takes place where there is active habitat management and predation control.

The Red-legged Partridge

The red-legged or 'French' partridge is indigenous to southern Europe and was first successfully introduced into Suffolk in the late 1700s. In the wild it is largely confined to the southern and eastern parts of Britain, although odd birds do turn up elsewhere from time to time.

Similar to the grey partridge in size, the red-legged partridge is a much brighter coloured bird, with strongly barred flanks and a distinctive black and white eye stripe. As with the grey partridge, there is little differentiation in plumage between cock and hen. Eggs are laid in late April and May and they hatch at the beginning of June. The chicks are far less reliant on insect food than those of the grey partridge, and so the red-legged partridge has weathered the changes in farming patterns rather better than its grey cousin.

As a sporting quarry, the red-legged partridge is often reckoned to be inferior to the grey, largely because it has a tendency to run rather than fly. However, it responds much better to artificial rearing, and large numbers of birds are therefore released each year for shooting.

The Red Grouse

Native only to Britain, the red grouse is a sub-species of the willow grouse, which inhabits both America and Eurasia. It lives on high ground, especially heather moorland, in Scotland, northern England and Wales. Red grouse are also found in Ireland, especially in the west of the country.

Compact and energetic, the red grouse is a skilled and powerful flyer, and quite distinctive in its dark rufous plumage which blends perfectly with the colour of the heather. It is recognised worldwide as a premier sporting bird, and attracts many shooters to Britain from overseas to sample the unique shooting that it provides.

Red grouse cannot be commercially reared, and proper habitat management is therefore essential if numbers are to be maintained. Grouse are very territorial, and like to nest in the security of deep old heather with younger heather nearby for feeding. The hen lays a clutch of 6–12 eggs in a heather-lined depression in the ground between late April and May, and the young chicks mature rapidly. Breeding success is often at the mercy of weather conditions and the presence of disease, and is therefore subject to sharp fluctuations from year to year. This means that grouse shooting is very unpredictable, and estates will frequently reduce shooting pressure or cancel shooting altogether if breeding has been poor.

The lone rough shooter can hunt at his own pace and in his own way.

CHAPTER 6
Rough Shooting

There is no easy definition of the term 'rough shooting', despite the fact that it encompasses the majority of the sporting shooting carried out in Britain today. Perhaps the simplest way to describe it is informal shooting which takes place over land not managed by a gamekeeper and where game is not deliberately reared and released. It involves the pursuit of a wide variety of different birds and animals, from game birds such as pheasants to wild ducks, woodpigeons, rabbits, hares and waders such as woodcock and snipe. The variety of the bag is matched by the variety of the countryside in which the rough shooter enjoys his sport. Farmland, woods, hedgerows, heaths, ponds, rivers, lakes, even derelict industrial land all provide exciting opportunities for rough shooting, giving many thousands of shooters the chance to hunt game, often at very little cost.

Clothing and equipment

Because it is an informal sport, the emphasis when choosing equipment and clothing for rough shooting should be on the practical. Most shooters rely on a single versatile 70 mm (2¾ in) chambered 12-bore shotgun. This is capable of handling a variety of cartridges to suit the quarry most likely to be encountered. A 30 g (1¹/₁₆ oz) or 32 g (1¹/₈ oz) game load of number 6 or 7 shot is sufficient to deal with most winged game, but if the main quarry is rabbits or hares, number 5 shot may be more

suitable. If there is a likelihood of getting a shot at a wild duck, then a slightly heavier load may be preferred in shot size 5 or 4, and for the chance opportunity at a goose, many rough shooters keep in their top pocket a couple of high-velocity cartridges loaded with number 3 shot.

The rough shooter generally has to walk in search of his quarry, so everything he needs to take with him must be carried, from cartridges to sandwiches. A cartridge belt is a very practical way of carrying ammunition, and it is a good idea to select one which has closed ends to the loops. This ensures that the cartridges are kept as clean and dry as possible. A good, stout game bag is very useful. The best types have a net front for carrying game so that it can cool quickly, and a waterproof inner compartment. Alternatively you may choose to carry one or two birds in a poacher's pocket in your coat or on a strap suspended from your belt. Remember, however, that everything you carry must be comfortable enough for you to be able to mount and swing your gun smoothly and shoot without effort should a pheasant suddenly rise or a rabbit bolt from the brambles in front of you.

In most situations the rough shooter is likely to encounter during a British winter, a pair of wellington boots is the best footwear, preferably with thick socks inside to prevent chafing. A practical pair of breeks or trousers in cord or moleskin can be complemented in wet weather by waterproof overtrousers with the bottoms worn outside your wellingtons. Overtrousers are especially useful when you are expecting to walk through thick, wet cover such as kale or sugar beet. For all the new fabrics and materials on the market, a thornproof, waxed cotton coat is still by far the most popular outer garment for rough shooting. It is tough, waterproof, practical and relatively cheap, its only major drawback being that it retains moisture inside from perspiration if the weather is warm or if you have a lot of hard walking to do. In these circumstances a cotton military-style tunic may be preferable. Whatever coat you choose, however, make sure that it is sufficiently roomy for you to mount and swing your gun easily. Tight clothing is constricting and uncomfortable.

A hat made from tweed, moleskin or waxproof cotton is important both to keep your head warm in winter and to ensure that your face is better hidden from the birds which you are trying to hunt. Finally, a pair of gloves or mittens can, on a cold day, make all the difference between comfort and misery. Cold hands make shooting difficult. They can even make it hazardous if fast, positive contact with triggers and safety catch is lost.

Hedgerow hunting

Perhaps the most popular form of rough shooting is simply walking-up hedgerows and

An informal day's rough shooting – a chance to relax in good company.

A varied bag is the hallmark of the rough shooter.

ditches in search of game, usually with the help of a gundog. Its enjoyment comes from the fact that the shooter can hunt at his own pace and in his own way, taking pleasure in the sights and sounds of the countryside and using his own skills and those of his dog to create the chance of a shot. On a hedgerow-hunting expedition the size of the bag is of little relevance. To the lone rough shooter, a single pheasant or pigeon stalked, flushed and killed after a successful shot is worth a dozen or more birds shot on a busy day by the driven game shooter.

Tactics for hedgerow hunting may vary, but one thing always remains constant, and that is the need for stealth, silence and careful observation. By using the natural cover of overhanging trees or undulations in the ground it is often possible to get close enough to a sitting rabbit or roosting pigeon to ensure that you get a shot the moment it dashes for cover or flaps frantically from its perch.

While pigeons will flush and rabbits will readily bolt at the sight of a human hunter, it is much harder to flush game birds such as pheasants or woodcock if you do not have a dog, and the relationship between the rough shooter and his gundog – particularly one he has trained himself – is something very special indeed. A good dog will tell his master when there is game about or, conversely, when there is no point in hunting out a partic-ular bramble bush any further. Learn to understand every message your dog is trying to give you and be on the spot the moment it feathers its tail and dives excitedly into cover, otherwise you could well miss the chance of a shot. Of course it is important to ensure that your dog hunts close to you. If it does not, then it may put up any amount of game, but the birds and beasts which it disturbs will more than likely be out of range. An endless succession of pheasants rising 40 metres away, ahead of an uncontrollable dog, is one of the most frustrating things that the rough shooter can experience.

Shooting with a companion

If there is no dog to flush them, game birds will frequently run ahead of the shooter as he walks along a hedge or ditch. Even if they do become airborne they can be extremely cunning, frequently rising on the opposite side of the hedge from the shooter. That is one of the reasons why it is a good idea to go shooting with a companion. It is far easier for two guns to cover every possible angle of escape for a pheasant than it is for a lone shooter to do so, and if you ensure that one gun walks on each side of the hedgerow, then no matter which way the bird flushes, one of you should have it covered.

Shooting with a companion, however, means that you must always be aware of your partner's position. You will often be working around thick patches of cover such as trees or bushes which will hide one shooter from the other. On top of this, it is quite likely that you will both be moving. The golden rule, therefore, is never to shoot where you can-not see that it is safe to do so. Do not shoot through hedges or undergrowth, or take a shot at a low bird flying in front of cover. You just never know what may be behind it. Ground game poses special risks since, of necessity, shooting at it involves taking shots at ground level. Never shoot at ground game unless you can clearly see all the ground around it.

It is all the more important to observe the rules strictly when you are shooting close to a public road or footpath. A passer-by, unaware that shooting is taking place nearby, can easily be alarmed or upset at the sound of shooting or at spent pellets falling around him. It is far better to let a pheasant, pigeon or rabbit go than to take a shot which, even though it might technically be safe, will nevertheless frighten or alarm a passer-by. Upsetting a member of the public will probably colour his or her view of shooters for many years to come, and may even do permanent damage to the reputation of shooting.

Rabbit shooting

The rabbit has long been one of the most important quarry species for the rough shooter. Rabbits are a serious agricultural pest because of the damage they do to growing crops, and they were almost wiped out in the 1950s when the disease myxomatosis was deliberately introduced to control their numbers. However, many rabbits have now become immune to myxomatosis and in recent years the population has greatly increased once again. Rabbits may be shot at all times of the year, and a good time to ambush them is on warm summer evenings when they are feeding some distance away from their warrens. The specialist rabbit shooter may well use ferrets to flush them from their burrows. In this case, it is likely that those burrows which cannot be covered effectively with a gun will have nets placed across them to catch the rabbits as they try to escape. Shooting when ferrets are working underground requires extra care, as a ferret may easily follow a rabbit out of the burrow as it bolts.

Shooting rabbits by night from the back of a vehicle has become very popular, and it is an extremely effective method of control. However, it can be hazardous if not done with great care. If you are planning to shoot from a vehicle, make sure that you have a firm, stable shooting position. Wear warm, comfortable clothing, and footwear which will give you a firm grip when you start shooting. Discuss with the driver beforehand how he intends to cover the ground, and shoot only those targets which are fully illuminated by the vehicle's headlights or a separate lamp. Never shoot from a fast-moving vehicle. It is a good idea to inform the police if you are likely to be shooting after dark, especially if it is within earshot of nearby houses. This will help to prevent any confusion should a local resident, unaware that you are carrying out rabbit control, report hearing shots close by at night.

Ferrets may be used to flush rabbits from their burrows.

Almost every type of countryside has rough shooting potential.

Snipe and woodcock

If the ground over which you are shooting has an area of wet or boggy land, particularly one where cattle have been grazing, then you might be lucky enough to get a shot at snipe. These small wading birds have long been prized by shooters, and present a particularly testing target as they zig-zag away when flushed. Moreover, though small, they are very good to eat.

Snipe prefer wet grassland with plenty of tussocky sedge and rushes. They are easily alarmed, and should therefore be walked-up with stealth. Try to approach potential snipe ground quietly and with the wind at your back. This will mean that the birds will have to take off towards you before they turn and fly away.

Although snipe breed throughout Britain, the snipe population is greatly augmented in winter by migrant birds arriving from Scandinavia and Iceland. However, because they need soft ground in order to feed for tiny invertebrates with their long, flexible bills, a prolonged frost will cause them to move south or west in search of milder conditions.

Another migratory bird which is often encountered by the rough shooter is the woodcock. Although technically a wader, it does not inhabit marshy ground like other wading birds. Instead it lives in mixed woodland and dense thickets interspersed with pasture, where it feeds on earthworms. The woodcock is traditionally regarded as a game bird and is highly prized by game shooters when it is flushed by the beaters on a pheasant drive. There are even shooting estates which specialise in woodcock shooting. These are mostly in the south-west of England and west Wales, where large numbers of migrant woodcock regularly overwinter.

Snipe

Many woods will hold a few woodcock. They can often be found in the densest part of the wood where there are a few evergreen shrubs such as holly or rhododendron bushes. When disturbed they will flit silently through the branches, and you will need to be very quick in order to get a clear shot. If you are shooting with a companion, then it is a good idea to work through any likely woodcock cover together, one walking on each side to maximise the chance of someone getting a shot should a woodcock be there.

The walked-up shoot

Although most rough shooters hunt alone or with a single companion, many rough shoots are more organised, bringing together a number of guns for a day's walked-up shooting. Farms which do not form part of a shooting estate very frequently organise a few days of walked-up shooting during the season, and the opportunity to join a group of other shooters for a friendly day's sport in the countryside is not to be missed.

As we have seen, a walked-up shoot is far less formal than a driven game shoot, but it can nevertheless mean a great deal of organisation and planning on the part of the host, and can often involve a considerable number of people. So if you receive an invitation for a day's walked-up shooting, make sure you return your host's courtesy by turning up at the meeting point on time, and with everything you need.

Imagine that you have become friendly with a local farmer and, knowing that you are interested in shooting, he has invited you to one of the regular shoots which he holds on his land for your first day's walked-up pheasant shooting. Before the big day you will have got ready all your shooting gear, making sure that everything is in good repair and that it will not let you down when you are out in the field. The equipment required is exactly the same as you would need for any

other day's rough shooting, but remember that you might be taking many more shots than you would on a hedgerow ramble, so put an extra box of cartridges into the car. Also, if you are walking through leafy crops like sugar beet or kale, you are likely to get very wet if you do not wear a pair of waterproof over-trousers or leggings. And do not forget your game bag. You may well have to carry what you shoot for some considerable distance.

At the farmyard where the shoot is meeting, there is a buzz of activity. Your host introduces you to the other guns, and very soon you are swapping stories and joking with them. Meanwhile your dog is doing exactly the same, for while on a formal driven shoot a dog may be an unnecessary distraction, when you are walking-up game, a good team of dogs is essential. Do not hesitate to take yours with you, provided of course that it is sufficiently well trained not to spoil the shooting for you or the other guns.

Once you have got your coat, boots and overtrousers on, and having left your spare cartridges in the car after checking that you will be coming back to the farmyard at lunch time, you climb aboard a farm trailer with the other guns and dogs or maybe squeeze into the back of a Land-Rover for the journey to the first drive, which is to be through a large field of sugar beet. On leaving the vehicle you remove your gun, broken, from its slip, and keep it open and unloaded until the drive actually starts. This way, everybody can see, even from a distance, that your gun is safe.

You are asked by your host to line out along the edge of the field. Because it is a big day, there are a number of beaters and dog handlers in the line as well as the guns, so your host makes sure that the non-shooters and dogs are evenly spread along the line, alternating with the guns. Then, at a given signal, you load and close your gun, remembering to keep the muzzles pointed at the ground in front of you, and the drive commences. As you walk, carry your gun in one of the

A walked-up shoot. Guns and beaters line out for the start of a drive.

accepted ways – either over your forearm, muzzles pointing down, or grasping the fore-end with one hand and the small of the stock with the other, with muzzles pointing safely upwards.

You are concentrating, of course, on keeping your footing as you walk through the thick sugar beet, and looking hard at the cover in front of you in the hope that very soon a pheasant might flush from it and give you your first chance of the day. But you must also keep a close watch on your neighbours to left and right in order that the line is kept straight. A straight line of guns is essential in walked-up shooting. If one individual forges ahead of the line or drops behind it, then he immediately reduces the safe angle of fire for those on either side of him. This is annoying for the other guns and indeed positively dangerous. If for any reason somebody has to stop, perhaps to retrieve a bird which has fallen behind the line, then the whole line must stop together. Only when everybody is ready can the drive recommence.

Perhaps the line of guns has to change direction, and you are asked to pivot on the left- or right-hand gun. Again, this manoeuvre must be carried out whilst keeping the line as straight as possible, the outermost gun performing an arc around the one at the other end of the line, who remains stationary until the manoeuvre is completed.

If you have a dog with you, then ideally, it should quarter the ground in front of you, hunting back and forth at a distance of 20 metres or so from the advancing line of guns. In this way, the maximum amount of cover can be tried for game, and there is far less chance of any bird escaping by sitting tight and waiting for the guns to walk past it. If, however, you are not sure of your dog's ability to quarter at close range, then it is better to keep it walking to heel unless it is actually retrieving. A dog which races forward

Guns and beaters at the start of a drive. Rough shooting is much more informal than driven game shooting.

out of control and flushes game 40 metres ahead of the line will spoil the drive for you and everyone else.

When, with a flurry of wings, a pheasant startles you by exploding from the beet just ahead, take the shot in as calm and measured a way as you can. Most walked-up birds will be going-away shots at a rapidly accelerating target. A first barrel fumbled through alarm or excitement may not leave you sufficient time to recover the situation with your second shot. Much better to let the bird get well into the air, steady yourself and read its line before pulling the trigger. Remember also that your pheasant is likely to be climbing fast. Blot it out with your barrels and keep your shot over it as it rises, and you will see it tumble satisfactorily into the beet ahead of you. The majority of going-away birds are missed underneath.

Stand and walk

A variation on the conventional walked-up day is one in which the guns take it in turns to stand and walk. At the start of the day you will split into two equal teams. One team will act as standing guns at one end of a piece of cover, while the other will line up at the other end in the conventional manner and walk it up towards them. At the next drive the teams will change places and those who have just done the walking will take their turn as standing guns. The stands are usually informally arranged, and there are no numbered pegs to go to, which of course makes it all the more important to listen closely to the instructions you are given before the beginning of the drive by the shoot organiser.

There are a couple of other points that need to be borne in mind when you are shooting in this way. As a walking gun you may be asked to leave any birds which fly forwards, so that they can be dealt with by the standing guns in front of you. Instead you will be paying attention to those which endeavour to break out of the sides of the drive or which curl back over your head in an effort to escape behind. Even so, you must remember that you are walking towards a line of guns who are possibly concealed behind a hedge, and that, as you approach the place where they are standing it is dangerous to take any low shot in front of you. Likewise, if you are standing, ensure that any bird you shoot at is high enough to avoid your shot endangering the walkers as they make their way towards you. If it is too low, then leave it for another day.

The lone rough shooter in a wintry fen embodies the true spirit of the hunter.

Reared mallard are sometimes released onto flight ponds to augment the wild population.

CHAPTER 7
Wildfowl Shooting

Ducks and geese offer some of the most exciting shooting in Britain. Apart from a limited number of mallard which are reared and released by shooting estates, almost all the birds which are encountered by the shooter as he patrols the marsh or waits beside the river or flight pond are absolutely wild. To hunt such a wary, keen-eyed and intelligent quarry successfully requires that you understand its behaviour and are willing to learn the techniques of fieldcraft necessary to enable you to get close to it or to bring it close to you. Above all, it requires an enthusiasm to seek out the wild places where ducks and geese gather, and to do so at times of day or night and in weather conditions in which most people want to be back at home and in front of the fire or tucked up in bed.

It is this connection between ducks and geese – known collectively as wildfowl – and the wild and lonely marshes, estuaries, rivers, lakes and fens that injects wildfowl shooting with a special magic which many shooters find irresistible. It is no accident that the sport has captivated generations of writers and artists.

Wildfowl may be shot either inland over rivers, flight ponds and freshwater marshes, or below the high-water mark over salt marshes and estuaries. Experienced wildfowlers will sometimes say that only coastal duck and goose shooting can properly be described as 'wildfowling', and that anything else is simply either 'duck shooting' or 'goose shooting'. It is true that real wildfowling requires great stamina and determination, and that to be a wildfowler you have to be prepared to face foul weather and difficult, even dangerous terrain. However, the mastery of wildfowling skills and a willingness to overcome wind, rain and cold is just as important on the bleak marshes above the sea-wall as it is on the foreshore, and although it is true to say that salt water and the ebb and flow of the tide add a dash of spice to wildfowling, it is unfair to brand inland shooting as a lesser sport.

What distinguishes all wildfowl shooting from other forms of sport with the shotgun is the fact that most of the ducks and geese shot by wildfowlers in Britain are migratory birds which breed in northern Scandinavia, Iceland and even arctic Russia, and which travel thousands of miles each autumn to their traditional wintering grounds. In the depths of winter, when the freshwater ponds and rivers are frozen and only the salt water remains open to wildfowl, vast numbers of migratory ducks, geese and waders may pack into the estuaries of Britain. The fact that migratory wildfowl are a resource which we share with other countries means that we have an international responsibility to care for and conserve the natural habitat on which they depend. That is why the most important wildfowl sites are designated under European law and international conventions. Wildfowlers take their responsibility for conservation very seriously indeed, and there are long-established links between the sport and the conservation movement.

Wildfowling takes the shooter to wild and lonely places.

Wildfowl identification

A knowledge and understanding of wildfowl and their habits is essential to success in wildfowling, whether above or below the sea wall. The first priority for the newcomer to wildfowling is to be able to recognise the quarry species he is likely to encounter in the area where he is planning to go shooting, and to be able to distinguish them from protected birds which may share the same habitat. Accurate quarry recognition is absolutely essential, and it must be perfected not only in broad daylight, but in the half-light of dawn and dusk, which is when most wildfowling takes place. Indeed, experienced wildfowlers will instantly be able to recognise their quarry from its silhouette, its call and even the sound of its wingbeats. To do this takes time, and although it is possible to learn a great deal

This shooter carries a mighty double 8-bore.

from a good book on bird identification, there is no substitute for patient hours of watching wildfowl in the company of an expert.

There are, however, certain points of guidance which will help you to distinguish between the various species. Ducks can be divided into two categories, namely diving ducks and surface-feeding, or 'dabbling' ducks. Divers feed on invertebrate creatures which they find at the bottom of deep water such as big tidal estuaries, reservoirs or deep ponds. They are characterised by a slightly dumpy appearance, and their legs and paddles are set far back along their bodies to assist them when swimming underwater. When in flight, diving ducks have a distinctively rapid

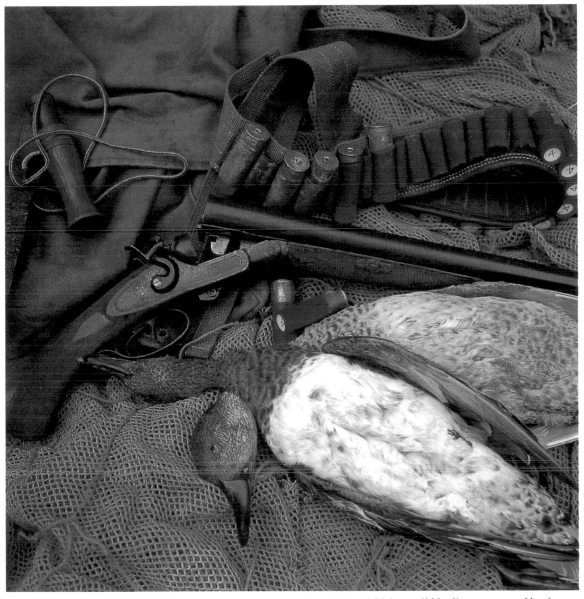

A traditional 10-bore wildfowling gun, capable of handling heavy loads at long ranges.

wingbeat. The diving ducks which may be shot are tufted duck, pochard and goldeneye.

Dabbling ducks feed on or from the surface of the water, or graze upon vegetation close to the water's edge. They have an elegant, streamlined outline, and are masters of the air. Most of the duck which are commonly shot by wildfowlers are dabblers, and because they tend to be vegetarian in habit, they make the best birds for the table. The mallard is the best known of the quarry species in this group, and is universally recognisable. Other species are the wigeon, pintail, gadwall, shoveler and the little teal, unmistakable because of its size.

The quarry geese comprise pink-footed and

white-fronted geese, both of which are entirely wild and migratory, the Canada goose, a feral species that has spread extensively from birds introduced to Britain in previous centuries to grace the ornamental lakes of great estates, and the greylag goose, Britain's only native breeding goose species. Canadas are easily distinguished by their great size, their long black necks and white cheek bars. The other species, or 'grey geese' are more easily identified in flight by their calls.

All wildfowl, of whatever sort, must be positively identified before they are shot at, and they must never be confused with protected birds. There can be no excuse for shooting at a protected species, and if there is any doubt in your mind whatsoever as to a bird's identity, then hold your fire.

Clothing and equipment

Wildfowl shooting is a specialised branch of the sport which calls for particular equipment and clothing. Because many of the shots taken at wildfowl are close to the maximum effective range of the conventional 12-bore shotgun, and because wildfowl are well protected by thick layers of feathers and down, it is best to select a gun which is capable of handling high-velocity loads of at least 36 g (1¼ oz). Many dedicated wildfowlers opt for a 12-bore magnum shotgun, proved for 42 g (1½ oz) or more, and a considerable number of devotees use 10-bore or 8-bore guns, especially when hunting wild geese. A wildfowling gun must be strong and robust, for it will have to operate in wet or muddy conditions. Below the seawall the salty atmosphere is particularly corrosive, and the foreshore is no place to take a fine, expensive shotgun.

Wildfowlers have traditionally used slightly larger shot sizes than game or rough shooters since, when coupled with the heavier loads of the standard wildfowling cartridges, they maintain more pellet energy – and thus duck-stopping power – at longer ranges. However, it must be remembered that if steel shot is being used, larger shot is also needed to compensate for the lower specific gravity of steel relative to that of lead.

Clothing for wildfowl shooting must be warm and waterproof. If you are planning to wait for ducks beside a pond or river after a day's rough shooting, then an extra sweater under your waxproof coat will probably suffice, but for serious wildfowling on the marsh or estuary you will need rather more than this. First, waders or thigh boots are essential. It is best to get a pair which is one or two sizes too big for you, and then to wear extra thick seaboot stockings, plus, if you like, a pair of quilted ankle-length 'wellie socks' for extra warmth. Do make sure, however, that your extra socks completely fill the spare space in the feet of your waders. If you try to walk across soft, estuarine mud in loose-fitting boots they will be sucked off in an instant, as many a novice wildfowler has learned to his cost. A pair of waterproof overtrousers will keep your bottom dry should you wish to sit down. A good plan is to cut the legs off at the knees, so creating a pair of waterproof 'shorts' which may be worn over your waders.

Keeping warm can be a problem when out wildfowling, as you may need to remain stationary for long periods. So when the weather is severe be sure to start off with clothing that retains your body's heat. The secret is to wear several thin layers under your waterproof coat. These will trap layers of air and provide excellent insulation without creating so much bulk that you are unable to mount and swing your gun. Remember also that while long underwear may not be the height of fashion in everyday wear, it is never out of place on the marsh. Indeed, most serious wildfowlers would not be without their long-johns and long-sleeved vests in midwinter.

A waxproofed coat or smock is an ideal outer garment, and it is sensible to add a

Keeping warm can be a problem when wildfowling in the depths of winter.

towelling choker in wet weather to keep the rain from trickling down your neck. As with rough shooting, a hat is essential to retain your body heat and ensure that your face can be hidden from wary wildfowl, and in cold conditions a pair of shooting gloves or mittens will be very welcome.

A capacious game bag is very useful when wildfowl shooting. It will be needed to carry all those extra little bits of kit which are necessary on the marsh, and it will also be useful to sit on. Moreover, it will come in handy if you should be so lucky as to shoot a duck or a goose. Choose one with two compartments; in this way you can keep wet, muddy things like camouflage nets and dead ducks separate from your sandwiches and Thermos flask.

Always carry a small torch in your bag. It can be invaluable when you are looking for a lost bird or trying to find your way home in the dark, and in an emergency it will help a potential rescuer to locate you. However, do not use it any more than is absolutely necessary, especially before morning flight, as a flashing light on the marsh will create an unnecessary disturbance. A pair of binoculars is very useful when out wildfowling, as it enables you to identify birds at long range, and so adds a great deal of extra interest to your visit to the marsh. There is no need for binoculars to be big and clumsy these days; a pocket-sized pair of roof-prism field glasses

A tide flight on the salt marsh. This wildfowler is using a camouflage net to help conceal himself in a creek.

of, say, 8 × 21 magnification is quite adequate. A penknife and a pull-through will help you with running repairs or removing mud from your gun barrels, while a long, stout wading stick will allow you to test the depth of the water as you cross flooded creeks or ditches. A whistle is also a valuable piece of safety equipment, while every sensible fore-shore wildfowler will carry a compass – and know how to use it. It is no joke to be lost on a strange marsh with a rising tide and a dense blanket of fog all about you. In these circum-stances, a compass can be a real lifesaver.

Flighting

The aim of most wildfowlers is to intercept ducks and geese as they travel between their feeding and their resting or roosting grounds. Under normal circumstances ducks feed at dawn and dusk, and roost during the day on open water or in the security of ponds or reed beds. Geese, on the other hand, feed during the daylight hours and roost at night, often on sandbanks exposed by the tide. Thus there is a natural traffic of wildfowl in the morning and evening, and these two spells of activity are known as morning flight and evening flight. The process of shooting wildfowl at these times, or at other periods of natural movement, is known as flighting.

To flight wildfowl successfully on the open marsh requires a detailed knowledge of the neighbouring feeding and roosting grounds, in order that you can position yourself underneath the anticipated flight line between the two. If there is a pond or lagoon where birds regularly come to feed, or from which they regularly depart at first light, or if there

is a river or main creek along which they prefer to fly, then use these features to guide you to a suitable flighting position. Take account of the wind direction, which may well make the birds deviate from their normal route. Wind strength is also very important to the wildfowl shooter, as ducks and geese will always fly lower in a strong wind. Indeed, a howling gale is something which the coastal goose shooter prays for, since it gives him his best chance to get within range of the mighty skeins as they battle over the foreshore where he is lying in wait.

Magic of the marshes. You must have your wits about you at flight time.

Having found a suitable position on the marsh or river bank, make sure that you are well hidden in a creek or ditch, in a clump of reeds or in a hide. Wildfowl are sharp-eyed and will quickly spot anything amiss on the marsh. If you do not conceal yourself sufficiently well, they will give you a wide berth.

Once in position, try to face the direction from which the birds are expected, but keep looking about you constantly. Remember that there is nothing guaranteed about wildfowl shooting, and ducks in particular may come from any direction, at all ranges, speeds and altitudes. You must have your wits about you at every moment during flight time. If you do spot a party of approaching wildfowl which you have positively identified as quarry birds, then keep down in your hide and remain perfectly still until the very last moment. Any unnecessary movement, or a glimpse of your face, is likely to send the birds wheeling away in search of a safer place to settle.

Arrive in plenty of time to get into position before flight begins, and remember that if you are shooting the morning flight, this will mean finding your place well before it starts getting light. Equally, do not leave the marsh until the flight is over and the birds have stopped moving or it is genuinely too dark to shoot. Unnecessary wandering across the marsh during flight time causes disturbance and is annoying and discourteous to other wildfowlers. However, if there is nobody else on the marsh then you may, of course, wish to change position to take advantage of a better flight line, and no conscientious wildfowler should object to you leaving your position in order to retrieve a wounded bird whilst the flight is in progress.

Apart from dawn and dusk, the natural cycles of tide and moon create other periods of wildfowl traffic. A daytime tide will flood the mudbanks where birds may be roosting and, if the wind is sufficiently strong to make the water choppy and uncomfortable, will force them to seek an alternative roosting site, perhaps in the marshes surrounding an estuary or on a nearby lake or reservoir. By exploiting this natural movement you may be able to enjoy a tide flight. It will of course be necessary for you to consult a local tide table to confirm exactly the time and expected height of the tide, but remember that both of these factors may be altered quite dramatically by strong winds. The main period of activity during a tide flight is when the principal roosts are flooding, often two or three hours before high water, so make sure you get into position early. You must also remember to leave the marsh in good time: a rapidly flooding tide may easily cut off your line of retreat.

Wildfowl will also flight at night under the influence of the full moon. Wigeon in particular feed by moonlight, and when the sky is veiled by a thin film of high cloud it is possible to shoot them at night. Adequate cloud cover is essential, for when duck are flying against the backdrop of a clear night sky, even under the brightest of moons, they will be completely invisible even if only yards away from you. Moon flighting is a very exciting and particularly magical sport, made all the more precious by the limited number of occasions each shooting season when it is possible. However, it demands excellent marsh skills and a complete mastery of wildfowl identification, and is not an activity recommended to the unaccompanied beginner.

Flight ponds

You may have access to a pond or lake where wildfowl come to feed when it gets dark. Flight pond shooting is very popular, not just with specialist wildfowlers, but also with rough shooters and game shooters, who can use a flight pond to add an extra dimension to their day's sport. Many flight ponds are deliberately fed with grain, potatoes or pulses in order to attract ducks to them, and then shot throughout the season. Such shooting should not be carried out more than once a fortnight, however, otherwise the ducks will start to associate the pond with danger and will desert it altogether.

Ponds which are shot regularly often have permanent hides built around their perimeters. These provide safe and comfortable shooting positions, and ensure that the guns are well hidden from approaching ducks. If you are invited to an organised flight pond shoot, make sure that your host tells you where any other neighbouring guns are situated. If there is more than one hide around the same pond, then take extreme care not to take low shots at ducks which are about to settle on the water if there is another hide anywhere near your line of fire. Remember that shot will easily ricochet off the water.

Flight pond shooting can be very fast and exciting, and it is not unknown for the very best game shots, after a day's pheasant shooting, to be completely thrown by teal

which zip over the tops of their hides at head height or mallard which swing over the willows and sideslip quickly down to the water in front of them. As with all wildfowl shooting in low light conditions, it is necessary to keep your wits about you, spot your birds early and if they are dropping fast, as is often the case with flight pond shooting, get your barrels well underneath them.

As the light fades, you may well only be able to pick out your birds against one particular patch of sky that is lighter than the rest, such as the afterglow above the western horizon. If so, focus all your attention on this point. Do not attempt to search about you for birds which, even if close by, are nevertheless invisible in the darkness. Concentrate instead on the one 'window' available to you, and shoot the moment the bird enters it.

While the wildfowler generally picks up his birds as he shoots them, picking up on an organised flight pond shoot is generally left until flight is over. Make a mental note, therefore, of the locations of any birds you have shot, so that nothing is left behind. And if by chance you should drop a bird onto the water and find that, although it is unable to fly, it is nevertheless a lively swimmer, it is quite in order for you to despatch it by firing a second barrel at it on the water *provided, of course, that it is safe for you to do so*. This enables you to put it in the bag rather than leaving it behind, wounded, to suffer.

Evening beside the pond. Flight ponds can provide fast and exciting sport.

Calls and decoys

Instead of merely putting your faith in the wind and weather and hoping that the birds will fly over you, it is possible to use fieldcraft skills to bring ducks or geese close to where you are hidden. Wildfowlers do this by using calls and decoys. A call imitates the sound of a duck or goose, and can be used to attract the attention of birds passing close by, to bring them within shooting range. Some skilled wildfowlers are able to reproduce the note of

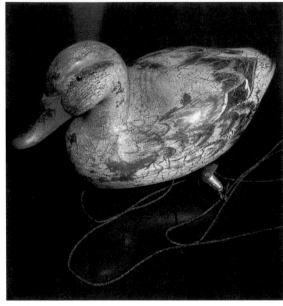

A traditional carved decoy from the USA.

Inland shooting over decoys.

Setting out decoys for a tide flight on the coast.

a duck or goose by using their voices entirely unaided, but most people use an artificial call, normally made of wood, plastic or metal. Calling can be very effective, but before you try it, spend some time listening to the natural vocabulary of ducks and geese as they feed and rest, then practise imitating the notes you hear.

Decoys at dusk. These decoys are rigged individually for shooting over flooded washes.

Use calls sparingly: do not overdo it and never call unless there are birds in the vicinity nobody, however proficient at calling, is able to conjure birds out of thin air. The real skill in calling is to be able to judge the exact moment when a single note will bring a duck or a goose wheeling round and looking for its comrades down below.

Calls are often used in conjunction with decoys. These are artificial ducks or geese, traditionally carved from wood but these days more commonly moulded in plastic. Wildfowl are naturally gregarious, and decoys exploit their desire to flock together with others of their kind. When placed in a natural-looking pattern on a suitable feeding ground, they can prove very effective at bringing birds down in front of the guns. Even three or four duck decoys can make all the difference in

encouraging passing birds to come in to a pond at evening flight, and some wildfowlers use dozens at a time to bring wigeon in to flooded washes.

Decoys are employed extensively by inland goose shooters, who position artificial full-bodied birds, shell decoys or even simple silhouette cut-outs on a field where the geese are known to feed regularly. By skilful decoying at dawn, when the geese are coming off the roosts to feed, it is possible to bring large numbers of grey geese right down in front of the guns to create one of the most exciting of all wildfowling opportunities.

When using decoys on water, remember that they will have to be 'rigged' with lines and anchor weights to prevent them from drifting away. Wildfowlers who regularly shoot shallow freshwater flashes often rig their decoys individually, as this offers more flexibility when building up a decoy pattern. When shooting on tidal or running water, it is generally more convenient to have several decoys rigged to a single line and anchor weight. By running the line back to the tide-line and pegging it securely, you can ensure that you can retrieve your decoys at the end of the flight, no matter how much the tide has risen.

A few well-positioned decoys can be deadly at bringing in single birds or pairs, but a larger rig of decoys is necessary when bigger packs of birds are on the move, and there is no doubt that the larger the number of decoys in your rig, the more pulling power it has. Those wildfowlers who shoot in locations where there may be large concentrations of genuine birds on the water only a short distance away know that it is pointless to take to the marsh with only two or three decoys in their bag, and prefer instead to employ all the decoys they can carry. In this respect, it is better to avoid the magnum-sized decoys with which the shooting retailer may tempt you. It is possible to carry two or three conventional birds for every one of these monsters, and the magnum decoys are in any case a nightmare to rig on the water in windy conditions. Two dozen full-bodied duck decoys will fit quite comfortably into a proprietary netting decoy-carrying bag, so a couple of fowlers shooting together are easily able to make a useful spread. Some fowlers who shoot where transporting decoys is not a problem regularly shoot with rigs of up to a hundred birds, and very effective they are too.

British wildfowlers have been slow to adopt the art of decoying, but they are now starting to realise the possibilities which it can bring to their sport. In doing so, they are borrowing a tradition from the United States, where the employment of big numbers of decoys by waterfowlers has a long and honourable history.

The wildfowler's dog

One of the most important players in the wildfowl shooting field is the gundog. While the game shooter can do without a dog of his own, and even the rough shooter might be able to get by much of the time without one, the wildfowler is hamstrung if he does not have a dog. When shooting on marshes, rivers, lakes or estuaries, there is going to come a time when a falling bird will come down in the water, and without a dog it is likely to be lost. Certainly there are some hardy souls who are prepared to strip off and swim for a bird, but how much easier and more comfortable it is to leave the retrieving to a good water dog.

At evening flight when there are wounded birds to be collected from reeds or thick waterside cover, a gundog is the only humane means of ensuring that they are quickly brought to hand and despatched, and it should be a point of honour with every wild-fowler at all times to have a dog to retrieve a bird which has fallen out of reach. To shoot a duck or a goose and then leave it unretrieved because you have no dog with you not merely runs contrary to the ethics of the sport of wildfowl shooting, it is a gratuitous waste of a valuable resource.

Wildfowl shooting opportunity

Wildfowl shooting inland has always been controlled, like every other form of sporting shooting, by landowners and occupiers. On the coast, however, there was historically a tradition of free shooting of wildfowl below the high-water mark. In Scotland, this tradition still is enshrined in ancient public right, provided that access to the shore can be gained by landowners' permission or by public right of way, and provided that local bylaws do not curtail it. In England and Wales, however, public rights of foreshore wildfowling are now a thing of the past.

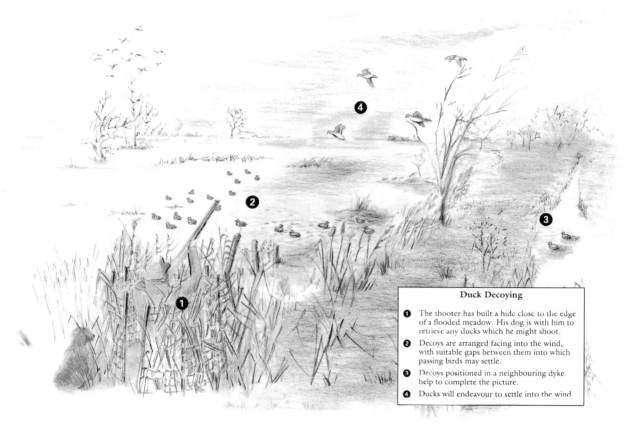

Duck Decoying

❶ The shooter has built a hide close to the edge of a flooded meadow. His dog is with him to retrieve any ducks which he might shoot.

❷ Decoys are arranged facing into the wind, with suitable gaps between them into which passing birds may settle.

❸ Decoys positioned in a neighbouring dyke help to complete the picture.

❹ Ducks will endeavour to settle into the wind

Nevertheless, wildfowling is accessible to any responsible shooter who wishes to try it, by virtue of the well-organised network of wildfowling clubs which own or occupy shooting rights in most of the principal coastal overwintering areas for ducks and geese. Most clubs are prepared to accept new members, and although it may be necessary for you to spend your first season watching and learning rather than shooting, you will get no better grounding in the sport than as a member of a wildfowling club. In addition to providing shooting opportunities for their own members, some clubs also make shooting permits available to non-members. Every principal club is affiliated to BASC, and for details of clubs and permit schemes operating in any particular area, you should contact them.

In areas frequented by migratory geese, shooting opportunities are eagerly sought after and jealously guarded. However, there are a number of expert professional guides who are able to take paying guests out goose shooting, and although the experienced wildfowler may be well able to find and shoot geese without professional assistance, the beginner is strongly advised to seek the help of a reliable guide. In Scotland, where much of Britain's wild goose shooting takes place, there is a registration scheme for goose guides which is operated by BASC and supported by the farmers, landowners and the police. The names of registered guides can be obtained from the BASC Scottish Office.

NAME THAT DUCK Here are some of the du

Mallard

The ubiquitous mallard is found throughout the northern hemisphere, and is the ancestor of all our farmyard ducks. With its bottle-green head, bright yellow bill, white neck-band and blue-and-white speculum, the mallard drake is immediately familiar. He is accompanied by his more soberly-hued mate, whose plumage is brown, but who still carries the blue-and-white speculum on her wings.

Mallard are found wherever there is water; on rivers, lakes, marshes and estu-

aries, and of course in urban parks, where they become very tame. They breed throughout Britain, producing 10–12 eggs on a down-lined nest hidden close to the water's edge at any time from midwinter onwards, though many early broods fail to survive to maturity. In winter, the 'home bred' population is augmented by very large numbers of migratory mallard from Scandinavia, Iceland and the Baltic.

Preferring to feed in shallow water, mallard eat a wide variety of vegetable food, from grain to the exposed stems of water plants. They will quickly take advantage of spoiled grain left in the fields after harvest and of frosted

potatoes. Like all ducks, they are masters of the air, but can easily be called by imitation of their quacking note, and by the use of decoys.

Teal

The little teal is the smallest of the commonly encountered ducks. Their diminutive size makes them instantly recognisable, and they can only be confused in the very early part of the shooting season with the protected garganey, a summer migrant. The drake teal has a grey back, a speckled breast and a gorgeous chestnut head with broad green eye stripe. His mate is brown, but shares his iridescent green speculum.

A few thousand pairs of teal breed in Britain, but the vast majority of birds which we see in winter are migrants, with many coming from Scandinavia, Russia and Iceland. They may be found together in large numbers, are very agile in flight, and when startled will rocket vertically into the air at great speed.

Teal are largely seed feeders, and prefer to dabble for the seeds of marsh grasses and sedges, though they will also take invertebrates, especially in summer. Their note, which they make in flight, is a soft but distinctive 'teep'.

nich the wildfowler is most likely to encounter.

Wigeon

Often considered the wildfowler's quarry *par excellence*, the wigeon is almost entirely a winter visitor to Britain, arriving from late August through to mid November from its breeding grounds in Scandinavia, northern Russia and Iceland. The cock is particularly handsome in his grey plumage with white underparts, pink breast and chestnut head with brilliant sulphur-yellow forehead flash, while the hen shares her partner's grey bill with black tip and metallic green and black speculum.

The wigeon is a grazing bird, which feeds on shallow flooded meadows and tidal flashes. It also occurs in large numbers where there is plenty of its favourite salt-water food, *zostera* or eelgrass. Wigeon are quick to exploit freshly flooded water

meadows in late winter, and where the habitat is right, tens of thousands of birds can congregate on a single site.

The familiar whistling call *wheeoo* is made by the cock birds both in flight and on the ground, while the hens contribute a low growling sound. Wigeon are very gregarious and, under the right circumstances, are easily decoyed.

Pintail

This elegant and strikingly beautiful bird is one of the most abundant duck species worldwide. The female shares the graceful, elegant shape of the drake, but her grey-brown coloration cannot compare with his handsome chocolate brown head and white neck stripes. Nor does she have the highly distinctive long and pointed black tail feathers from which the species derives its name.

Pintail breed in a few isolated sites in Britain, but are mainly winter migrants, arriving in the autumn from western Scandinavia, northern Russia and Iceland, to overwinter mainly on coastal sites around the major estuary systems, particularly in the west of the country. The pintail feeds largely on aquatic plant material, but also takes invertebrates such as water insects, molluscs and worms.

The species is very familiar to the wildfowler, and can easily be recognised in flight by its long outstretched neck and its long tail, coupled with its black and white coloration.

SPOT THAT GOOSE

These are the geese which the wildfowler is most likely to encounter.

Greylag goose

Britain's only native breeding wild goose species, the greylag is the ancestor of most of our domestic geese. It occurs throughout the western palearctic zone, through central Siberia to Japan, although most of the migratory greylags arriving in this country in the autumn breed mainly in Iceland, with a few birds coming from western Scandinavia and the Baltic coast. Home-bred greylags tend to remain fairly local in their habits, with significant concentrations of birds staying resident in the area where they were raised.

It is not easy to visually distinguish the greylag from the other grey geese at a distance, although identification marks to watch for are the pale grey-brown plumage of the head and neck, which extends down over the breast, and the orange-pink bill. Its voice, however, is distinctive: a deep bell-like *aang ung-ung*, which it makes in flight.

Natural grazers and foragers, greylags are partial to a wide range of agricultural crops, from grass through root crops and potatoes to winter cereals, something which brings them into conflict with the farmer, but which can also present decoying possibilities to the wildfowler.

Pinkfooted goose

A species which never fails to stir the fowler's heart when it arrives in the autumn from its breeding grounds in Spitzbergen, Iceland and Greenland, the pinkfooted goose or *pinkfoot* is the smallest of our grey geese, and together with the greylag, one of the two which the wildfowler will be most likely to encounter.

It can be distinguished from the greylag by its size, by its browner head and neck, and by its pink and brown bill. In flight, however, its characteristic call, a bright *ink-ink*, is a ready point of identification.

Like the greylag, it feeds largely on farmland, close to traditional coastal roosting sites such as the northern firths, the Tay and Forth valleys, the Lancashire coast and the Wash. It readily takes gleanings off the autumn stubbles before turning to grass, winter cereals and roots. Where vegetables are grown, pinkfeet also feed on carrots and a variety of brassica crops, often in very large flocks. Inevitably this brings them into conflict with agriculture.

Canada goose

Nobody could possibly mistake the massive Canada goose for anything else. It is our biggest quarry bird, and with its black neck, white cheek patches and grey-brown body plumage, it is immediately recognisable. In flight, Canadas make a distinctive *a-honk* note, which carries over long distances.

This goose is not native to Britain, but was introduced from America in the 1600s as an ornamental bird. It spread from the park lakes where it was first released, and has now become well established throughout the country. In particular it has exploited as breeding sites many of the newly created lakes that have resulted from gravel extraction. The species is also commonly seen in city parks. Although Canadas in their native country are migratory, British populations tend to stay close to where they were raised.

Canadas feed largely on grass, and are very domineering birds. This makes them unpopular with park owners, who increasingly express concern at the way they damage and soil the lawns around ornamental lakes. However, moves to curb the population have largely failed, and the Canada is on the increase.

TIDE GUIDE

Anyone who wants to go wildfowling on the coast must first understand how the tides work.

The tidal cycle is controlled by the gravitational forces which the moon and sun exert on the earth's oceans. Except in certain local circumstances, the tide rises and falls twice in each twenty-four hour period, with the exact time of high water advancing around three-quarters of an hour each day.

The height of the tide also varies throughout the month according to the phases of the moon, with the highest tides or 'spring tides' occurring a day or so after full moon and new moon, and the lowest tides or 'neap tides' occurring after the first and last quarters. At certain times of the year, in spring and autumn, particularly high tides will occur.

Tidal heights and predictions are given in local tide tables which should be obtained for the area in which you plan to shoot. Tables can usually be bought from yacht chandlers. Remember that the times and heights of tides can be greatly influenced by wind and weather conditions.

Make sure you understand the tides before shooting on the coast.

CHAPTER 8

Pigeon Shooting

The control of farm pests has always been an important aspect of shooting, and if the rough shooter obtains his sport by courtesy of a local farmer, then the killing of rabbits or winged vermin is one way in which he can assist his host. The control of one farm pest, however, has grown into a specialised form of shooting in its own right, where sporting enjoyment is as important as the need to protect crops. Pigeon shooting may be looked upon by the arable farmer as a means of defending his fields against the depredations of the grey flocks, but thousands of shooters recognise it as a uniquely challenging sport in which fieldcraft and first-rate shooting skills must be combined.

The need for pest control

Pigeons are recognised as Britain's number one bird pest on the farm. Indeed, the Ministry of Agriculture's scientists believe that in some cases the pigeon wreaks more devastation even than insect pests. On the important and valuable break crop of oilseed rape, it is not unknown for farmers to experience losses of up to 40 per cent of their final expected yields as a result of attacks by pigeons. Other brassica crops such as cabbages and Brussels sprouts are equally susceptible to pigeon damage, and even if their yield is not greatly depressed, pecking and the depositing of droppings by feeding pigeons will almost certainly mean that a vegetable crop is unsaleable.

The scale of the damage to individual crops is greatly influenced by the timing of a pigeon raid. Major concentrations of birds grazing on rape between November and early January appear to make little difference to the tonnage of rapeseed which finds its way into the combine harvester. Grazing from late January to March, however, is much more serious, and it is at this stage of late winter and early spring that most of the long-term damage is done.

Pigeon damage to young cabbages. Woodpigeons are Britain's number one farm bird pest.

Shooting of even very large numbers of pigeons probably has little overall effect on the bird's population, but at the level of the individual farm, it can be very effective in keeping pigeons from feeding on a particular field, and it is for this reason that many farmers welcome responsible pigeon shooters, especially those who are prepared to turn out at a moment's notice when crops are under siege.

Quarry species

The central character on the pigeon shooting scene is the woodpigeon, sometimes referred to as the ring dove, and recognisable by the white patches on each side of its neck and its white wing bars. A woodpigeon's flight is deceptive. One moment it may appear to be flapping lazily towards you, but the instant it spots danger it will jink and accelerate away with a display of aerobatic expertise which will defy even the most experienced of shots. Pigeon shooters may also encounter feral pigeons. This legal quarry bird is bred from generations of domesticated pigeons which have been released or which have escaped from captivity. It is smaller than the woodpigeon and has a wide variety of markings. Feral pigeons may cause considerable crop damage, but the shooter should only tackle them when they are actually raiding the farmer's crops, as they are indistinguishable from the domestic birds from which they were descended, and it is all too easy to shoot a valuable racing or domestic pigeon which has the misfortune of flying over your hide. For this reason, most pigeon shooters wisely concentrate their attention solely on woodpigeons.

The only other species which may legally be shot is the collared dove, a bird of the farmyard and grain store which feeds on spilled grain. It is a delicately built bird with a pale cinnamon colouring and a distinctive dark collar around its neck.

Tactics and timing

Pigeon shooting is geared closely to the farming calendar. In winter, as we have seen, it is the brassica crops which attract pigeons in large numbers. When there is snow on the ground and they are really hungry, they may feed on any brassica crop which is exposed above the snow. Brassica leaves, however, have a relatively poor food value, and it takes a pigeon a considerable time to eat and digest the amount of leaf material necessary to provide it with the energy it needs to survive.

At other times of the year this energy is much more readily obtained from other sources. In spring, fresh sowings of cereals, peas and beans are irresistible to pigeons, and they will eat not merely those few seeds which are left lying on the surface of the field by the drill, but will dig along the rows and remove large numbers. Newly germinated peas are also raided mercilessly by pigeons.

In summer, they will feast off fields of ripening cereals, especially barley or wheat which has been laid, or knocked over, before harvest by strong winds or heavy rain, and the moment the corn is cut, pigeons will descend on the stubbles to mop up the spilled grain. Then, when the autumn cultivations start, they can be seen on the newly sown crops of autumn cereals.

Each of these situations provides an opportunity for the pigeon shooter, for pigeons are truly a year-round quarry. It therefore pays to know and understand the patterns of cropping in the area where you intend to shoot, and to observe closely what the birds are feeding on at any one time. If you try to shoot over one crop while the pigeons are feeding on something entirely different, you will have a very frustrating time, and you will be unlikely to shoot many pigeons.

Clothing and equipment

A rough shooter's standard clothing and

equipment will in most cases be entirely suitable for pigeon shooting. A conventional 12-bore double-barrelled gun is ideal, although many shooters who operate out of the confined space of a pigeon hide prefer the convenience of a semi-automatic or pump-action gun, which does not have to be broken for reloading. Bear in mind that when you are pigeon decoying for extended periods, you may well be firing quite large numbers of cartridges, so ensure that the gun is a comfortable fit, and that recoil is not excessive with the cartridge that you are proposing to use.

A pigeon shooter's clothing will need to be appropriate to the prevailing weather conditions. In midwinter, conventional winter rough shooting kit will be required, with perhaps an extra sweater if you are expecting to be seated motionless in a hide for long periods. Likewise in high summer, you may find that you are shooting in shirt sleeves. If so, ensure that your shirt is of an appropriately sober colouring, and if necessary wear a skeet vest to assist with gun mounting and to make shooting more comfortable against the shoulder.

A hat is, of course, essential, and some shooters go so far as to wear a face mask or veil. These are certainly extremely effective, but they can also be very uncomfortable and awkward to shoot in unless you are used to them.

Decoying

Although most shooters will at some time in the season shoot the odd pigeon whilst walking along a hedgerow, standing at a pheasant drive or even crouching in a creek or on a salt marsh, the vast majority of pigeons are shot over decoys. Like wildfowl, they are gregarious by nature, and like to feed in the company of their fellows. Decoying exploits this habit by creating an illusion of a contented flock of birds feeding happily on their favourite food, the object being to invite any passing pigeon to join in the feast. Pigeons, however, are not stupid, and the decoy picture must be totally realistic if it is to do its job.

As we have seen, it is no use spreading your decoys over a crop on which the pigeons simply do not wish to feed. Nor is there any point in positioning decoys in a place where there is no passing pigeon traffic to spot them. It is essential before committing yourself to decoying in one particular spot to establish exactly where the flight lines are that the pigeons are using as they travel back and forth between their feeding grounds and the resting sites such as tall hedgerow trees and small copses, where they sit quietly to digest their food.

Timing is as important as geography. There is no point in trying to tempt pigeons down from the sky when there are none there in the first place. They feed at certain times of day, and only when they are actually interested in feeding will you draw them down to the decoys. During the short, dark days of winter this is not so much of a problem, since the birds will most likely need to spend the greater part of the daylight hours gathering whatever food is available, especially if that food is of relatively low nutritional value. At other times of the year, however, feeding periods are concentrated at different times of the day. Pigeons normally like to feed first thing in the morning, just after dawn, following which there is a spell of inactivity before the main feeding session starts, often at around midday. They then normally feed throughout the afternoon, putting in a particularly active burst of gorging before they go up to roost at dusk. Of course these times may vary according to local conditions, the weather and the quality of the feeding available, but the most consistent time for decoying is probably from midday through to the late afternoon.

When setting out decoys for pigeons, your aim will be to reproduce as closely as possible

Dead birds should be carefully set out to look like feeding pigeons.

When setting out your decoys, keep most of them with their heads to the wind.

the picture of a carefree flock of feeding birds. Most pigeons feed facing into the wind, and although you should not position your decoys in too regimented a manner, the majority should indeed be head to wind. They should also be well spaced out, leaving one or more inviting 'holes' into which guests can drop. Your aim will be to invite passing birds to come in to a killing zone around 25 metres from your hide.

There is no doubt that the best decoys are dead birds, and many serious pigeon shooters keep a few preserved and mounted pigeons to act as the main body of their decoy pattern, or use birds which they have shot a day or so previously. Some older shooters also still swear by wooden decoys which they have carefully crafted and painted themselves. Most, however, will have to opt for the next best thing, which is to use commercially available artificial decoys, of which there are several excellent styles, ranging from the full-bodied plastic type to the shell decoy, which, although it looks less realistic, has the advantage of being lighter and taking up less space in your decoy bag.

Top to bottom: shell decoy, full bodied plastic decoy, natural bird.

Shell decoys are light and take up the minimum of space.

In many situations artificial decoys will do an excellent job, but in strong sunlight their shiny upper surfaces do tend to reflect more light than a genuine bird, thus sending a warning signal to any approaching pigeon that something is not quite right. It is possible to overcome this by cutting the wings off a dead pigeon and glueing them to your artificial bird. Although it may sound a little strange, this trick works very well for many shooters. As your tally mounts during the course of a shoot, you should replace your artificial decoys with dead birds.

Whatever decoys you are using, however, it is important to ensure that they are easily visible from the air. This is achieved by mounting them on short sticks so that they are not hidden by the crop on which they are supposed to be feeding. Some proprietary decoys will rock back and forth in a gentle breeze when mounted like this, simulating a realistic pecking action. Likewise, each dead bird should be carefully set out to look like a feeding pigeon, its head supported either by a short forked twig or by a longer pointed stick pushed into the base of its lower mandible.

The white wing markings which a pigeon displays as it settles act as a powerful signal to any birds which might be watching that there is food to be had, and pigeon shooters seek to exploit this fact by using a cradle. This device consists of a long springy stem topped by an arrangement of wire into which a dead pigeon may be fixed with its wings spread. When correctly positioned in the cradle, the dead pigeon looks exactly as though it is just about to touch down amongst the rest of the decoy pattern. In addition, the lightest of breezes will make it rock realistically.

Apart from a little rocking in the wind, a decoy pattern is basically static creation, and the addition of movement can often provide the final touch which draws in the birds. As with the static cradle, the object is to simulate a pigeon which is just settling to feed amongst its contented fellows, and this can be achieved by placing a dead bird in one of the flapper cradles available through shooting retailers or from specialist pigeon shooting mail order companies. They are pegged out in the middle or around the edge of the decoy pattern, and can be operated by a string running back to the hide. When the shooter pulls the string, the wings of the dead pigeon open and close, exposing the white wing bars in a flash of movement calculated to attract the attention of any passing pigeon. However, technology is always on the move in pigeon shooting, and electrically operated flappers and rotating 'pigeon magnets' are now very popular. No matter what device you choose, however, do not over-use your pigeon flapper. It is most effective against a

bird passing across the far side of the field, well away from the decoys. Once a pigeon has committed itself to coming in for a closer look, leave the flapper well alone. And if you do not want to go to the expense of buying one, you can always try the old trick of lobbing a dead pigeon out of the hide and into your decoys just as a likely looking bird is passing by. However, if you are to make this work, your timing must be perfect.

A further refinement to the decoy pattern is the addition of 'lofters', pigeon decoys

Coming in to land. A dead pigeon in a cradle is a realistic imitation of a bird about to settle amongst the decoys.

mounted in high trees or on purpose made poles close to your spread. These simulate the birds which have enjoyed a tasty snack and are digesting their food before dropping down once more to rejoin their comrades. Lofters are easily visible to passing pigeons, and act as a signal to them to take a closer look. There are two ways of lofting decoys. The first is by throwing a weight attached to a length of strong fishing line over a convenient branch, then attaching a full-bodied decoy to the other end of the line and pulling it up into position before tying it off. The second is by using sectioned lightweight aluminium lofting poles. Lofters are effective, but take extreme care if you are using them anywhere near overhead power lines.

Hide construction

Attracting passing pigeons is only half the decoying story. The other is ensuring that you are perfectly concealed until it is too late for the visiting pigeon to discover that it has made a very bad mistake. Hide construction is therefore an integral part of the fieldcraft associated with pigeon shooting. The best possible hide is a natural one composed of materials which are to be found in the field where you are decoying, or one which simulates something which the pigeons will not associate with danger. The simplest is a hedgerow hide, which can be created in a few moments with a billhook, but check first that your farmer host is happy for you to do this. Alternatively he may be prepared to deposit a number of straw bales in the field, with which you can construct the warmest and most luxurious of all pigeon hides, a bale hide, which the birds will take for nothing more than a harmless straw stack. A variant of this at harvest time is to shoot from a parked farm trailer loaded with straw bales, a fortress of a hide which gives you the added advantage of height.

If you are unable to use natural materials, then you will have to bring your own hide, and the most common ones use a set of portable hide poles and a camouflage net. These can be very effective under most circumstances, although if it is very windy the camouflage netting can flap alarmingly. Make sure also that it is of a colour which matches the surrounding herbage. A dark olive green net will stick out a mile against the pale straw colours of dead winter grasses.

Whatever you make your hide of, however, ensure that it has a high back so that when you rise to shoot, your head is not silhouetted against its rim. If you do not take this simple precaution, then the jack-in-the-box effect as you bob up to take a shot will instantly startle the approaching bird, so presenting you with a far more difficult shot than might otherwise have been the case.

Surprisingly, pigeons will often take little notice of the sound of your shooting, provided that you remain well hidden. Most experienced pigeon shooters will confirm that if one bird is killed while a second is coming in to the decoys, the following bird will take no notice of the noise and can hopefully be bagged too if the shooter remains concealed. It seems that, with today's widespread use of gas bangers for bird scaring, pigeons do not necessarily connect loud bangs with danger, and can mistake a bird falling to your shot for one which is simply eager to land and feed.

Retrieving pigeons

You should pick up your dead birds regularly during a shoot. While dead pigeons when properly pegged out make the most effective decoys, when crumpled on the ground amidst a heap of white feathers they are likely to send the wrong signals to any approaching birds. When the coast is clear, retrieve them, and if there is a lull in the action, set them out amongst your decoys, either in addition to the artificial ones, or as replacements for some of them. It goes without saying that if you have a wounded bird down on the ground in front of you, you must go out and despatch it immediately, whatever other pigeon traffic might be following it.

A pigeon hide is one place in the shooting field in which it is not always necessary to have a gundog. Indeed, many experienced pigeon shooters prefer not to have their hide encumbered by a dog, especially when they are decoying over bare, freshly drilled fields where there is no cover in which a fallen bird may be lost. In other circumstances, however, humanity dictates that a dog should be available in order to quickly find any wounded bird which is not easily visible. Even then, some farmers might be unhappy about

pigeon shooters' dogs hunting for missing birds amongst fields of lodged cereals before harvest. If your farmer host says that he definitely does not want you to bring your dog, then you must try to ensure that every bird is killed cleanly, and avoid taking anything but the easiest of shots. Alternatively, there is no dishonour in declining the invitation to shoot; the woodpigeon may be an agricultural pest, but it still deserves your respect, and should not be allowed to lie wounded and unrecovered.

Lofting decoys in a hedgerow tree with the aid of fishing line.

Some shooters still swear by their own hand-carved wooden decoys.

Pick up your birds regularly. Stray white feathers from a dead pigeon will warn incoming birds that something is amiss.

Pigeon's eye view. This shooter is well concealed.

Roost shooting

Although it is not nearly so effective as decoying when it comes to killing large quantities of pigeons, roost shooting is a branch of pigeon shooting which offers superb sport. It is done in the late afternoon and evening as the birds, having finished feeding for the day, return to roost in woodlands close to their feeding grounds. Roosting woods can easily be identified through a little local reconaissance, and if you have one on your shoot or can obtain permission to shoot in one from the farmer or landowner, then make sure that you try this exciting form of the sport.

Organised roost shoots are often held in February, shortly after the end of the game shooting season, and when there are shooters operating in most of the local roosting woods and the pigeons are thus kept on the move, shooting can continue until it is dark.

Even within a favoured wood, there will be certain trees or groups of trees in which the pigeons will prefer to roost, and you should try to identify these before going shooting. A block of evergreen conifers in a mixed woodland is often sought after by pigeons, since it provides extra warmth and shelter, especially during bitter winter weather. Tall groups of trees are also favoured, as they make excellent vantage points from which the birds can spot danger.

Having located a likely-looking part of your roosting wood, and having got there well before dusk, try to find a spot where you can stand with your back to a tree and shoot through a gap or opening in the woodland canopy. When the roosting flight commences, try to spot your birds as they approach and take them as they zip across your gap – easier said than done, especially in a strong wind.

An important point to remember when roost shooting is to try to ignore the tracery of twigs and branches around you and concentrate only on the pigeon at which you are aiming. If you swing with the bird and shoot through the twigs, the chances are that you will be successful. Do not, however, try to shoot at birds which are out of range. Too often inexperienced pigeon shooters blast away at birds which are far above the treetops and way out of range. This only serves to scare off any birds which may be following, spoiling the sport of any other shooter waiting nearby. It is also a pointless waste of cartridges.

A good time to shoot roosting pigeons is in snowy weather. They will be particularly anxious to tuck well into the roosting woods and may come up to roost in large numbers. Like other birds, they also tend to find snow dazzling and disorientating and so will often fail to spot a waiting pigeon shooter. A windy evening can also be a very good time to go roost shooting, as the wind tends to keep the birds constantly on the move.

At all times when roost shooting remain quiet and still, keeping yourself as well camouflaged as possible amongst the trees. A few strands of camouflage netting may help you if there is little natural cover on the woodland floor. If by any chance a pigeon should settle within range of where you are standing, then remember that one of the objects of pigeon shooting is pest control, and so do not hesitate to shoot. However, make sure you aim for the feet, as otherwise you will see your 'sitter' fly off into the sunset.

The best hide is a natural one, built from local materials.

Try to let the birds come into the killing zone over your decoys before shooting.

Roost shooting offers superb sport.

In the days of the flintlock, pointing dogs were needed to find and flush game.

CHAPTER 9
Gundogs

Dogs have been among man's closest hunting companions since the dawn of time. At the end of the last Ice Age, domesticated dogs were being used by the ancient peoples of Europe to assist with hunting and with the guarding of livestock, and over the centuries their basic instincts to find, chase, catch and carry game have been carefully refined and channelled by generations of selective breeding. Fundamental to the dog's value as a hunting partner are its speed and the fact that its sense of smell is infinitely more powerful than that of a human being. Dogs are therefore able to locate game at a distance by detecting its airborne smell or 'scent', and to hunt animals or birds by following the scent trail that they leave on vegetation or on the ground.

This wonderful combination of speed and scenting ability was brought to perfection with the development of hunting hounds, which were – and still are – bred to hunt in packs in order to pursue and kill game. Other hunting dogs, the gaze hounds, were bred to bring down their quarry by speed alone. Their modern descendants are breeds like the greyhound and saluki. A third type was required for the ancient sport of falconry, where it was necessary firstly to locate game and then flush it on command for the hawk or falcon to chase, and it was from the pointing dogs bred by the old-time falconers that many of our modern gundog breeds descend.

The introduction of the sporting gun led to the requirement for many more dogs capable of using their powerful noses, their agility and their perseverance to find and flush game and then to retrieve the dead birds or animals after they had been shot by the hunter. These tasks of finding, flushing and retrieving game are still the basic requirements expected of a gundog, and over the last 200 years they have been refined by sportsmen and dog breeders to produce the wealth of specialist breeds we have today.

Why gundogs are needed

Gundogs are central to the shooting scene. In a practical sense, a dog is essential in order to locate birds or animals lurking in thick cover and then to flush them so that the guns are able to get a shot. Without a dog to hunt them out with its nose, many game birds would simply crouch low in the undergrowth and would never be spotted by guns or beaters. Hunting and flushing dogs therefore make a major contribution to the shooter's chances of putting game in the bag, and without the presence of one or more well-trained dogs, anyone wishing to shoot in even the relatively light cover of a grouse moor will be at a big disadvantage.

One of the objects of shooting is to produce food for the table, so when the bird or animal is shot, it has to be found and retrieved. That may be an easy task if it is lying dead in an open field beside your peg on a driven shoot. More often, however, it will have fallen in the depths of some thicket or maybe into the middle of a tidal river, and to recover it without a dog could mean hours of patient searching or a long, cold swim. Perhaps more importantly, it will sometimes happen that a bird or animal is only wounded by your shot. Wounded game is surprisingly strong, especially when only lightly struck in the wing. It will often run or swim a long way from where it first fell, and will almost always be impossible to find without a retrieving dog. Not only is it pointless to go shooting without being able to pick up what you shoot, it is inhumane to fail to make every effort to find and despatch wounded game, and a gundog is by far the most practical way of ensuring that, so far as is possible, you bring everything you shoot safely to hand.

But of course a dog is far more than a mere practical tool. It is a companion that will share with you the triumphs and disappointments of your shooting expeditions, a partner that will bring a new dimension to your rambles through fields and hedgerows, an indispensable member of the team. A dog will add to the excitement and sense of expectation as it eagerly greets you on a shooting morning, and in the evening when guns are cleaned and put away, it will join you as you relax and relive the day's happenings. Throughout your shooting career, a gundog will increase the pleasure you get from your sport many times over.

English Springer spaniels at work. The perfect rough shooter's dog, English springers also make excellent retrievers.

Gundog roles

As we have seen, there are three basic tasks which gundogs perform: finding game, flushing it, and retrieving it after it is shot. These tasks create a number of convenient groups within which the gundog breeds can be classified. By far the most commonly encountered in the shooting field today are the spaniel and retriever breeds, which are used for a wide variety of rough shooting, game shooting and wildfowling. Pointers and setters are to be seen mostly on the grouse moors, while the continental hunt-point-retrieve breeds are undergoing a remarkable rise in popularity and are increasingly finding favour, especially amongst rough shooters.

Dogs for finding and flushing game

The job of the spaniel is to hunt game from dense undergrowth and to flush it over the guns. Spaniels are therefore lively and energetic dogs which hunt busily through the thickest cover. Their long, tough coats offer surprisingly good protection against the roughest thorns and brambles, but their tails are normally docked to prevent the ends from becoming sore and damaged while they are hunting.

By far the most popular spaniel in the shooting field today is the English Springer Spaniel, bred to flush or 'spring' a wide variety of game. It is the ancestor of most of the other spaniel breeds, and its willing, active temperament and great versatility make it the perfect companion for the rough shooter. The English Springer is at its very best in the beating line, nose down and busily searching for game. However, it can also make a first-class retrieving dog, and in practice the rough shooter's spaniel is normally a dual-purpose animal which hunts out game and then retrieves when it is called upon to do so. There are many excellent blood lines available, so if you are looking for an English

Above: *Cocker spaniel.*
Below: *Working Cocker.*
This breed has developed distinct working and show strains.

Springer puppy, it will not be difficult to find a good working litter. English Springers stand up to 50 cm in height, and have brown and white or black and white coats. A white tip is often left on the tail, which helps the handler to see where his dog is working in dark, dense woodland.

The smaller Cocker Spaniel originated in the early 1800s in Wales and south-west England, where it was used to hunt woodcock. Cockers are busy little dogs, though not as powerful as English Springers. Like them, however, they have long, weather-resistant coats and very good scenting abilities.

Standing at around 40 cm in height, the Cocker has become a popular companion dog. Because most of the dogs kept as pets or for the show ring do not work in the shooting field, there has developed over the years a distinct difference between the working and the show strains of this breed. To their credit, some show breeders have done their best to ensure that their dogs retain the ability to hunt game, but if you are choosing a Cocker for shooting, then it is sensible to select a puppy from proven working parents.

Originating as early as the 1500s, the Welsh Springer Spaniel probably shares a common ancestry with the English Springer, but is rather smaller and has a more finely shaped

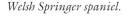
Welsh Springer spaniel.

Sussex spaniel.

Bred by the second Duke of Newcastle in the late 1700s at his Clumber Park estate in Nottinghamshire, the Clumber Spaniel comes originally from French stock. It is a large, bulky dog with a massive, square head and deep jowls. White with lemon markings, it is a slow, patient and methodical worker, and although Clumbers may take a long time to mature, some dogs are very reliable workers with very good scenting abilities.

Retrieving dogs

It is the task of the retriever to find and bring game back after it is shot. Because their primary job does not involve dashing about, finding and flushing unshot birds, the retriever breeds thus tend to be rather more sedate in temperament than the lively spaniels. That, however, does not make them any less loyal and dedicated workers. Most retriever breeds have an easygoing nature which makes them ideal family dogs.

Without doubt the most popular of all the retrieving dogs is the Labrador Retriever. Bred from stock originally introduced into Britain from North America, the Labrador is a compact dog standing 55-60 cm high, with a smooth, dense, waterproof coat, a kind and intelligent face, a powerful chest and a characteristic otter-like tail. It has an excellent nose with which to hunt and find shot game, and a placid temperament which makes it especially good as a family dog. Labradors are often the first choice of the game shooter who wants a dog which will sit quietly and patiently throughout a drive and then eagerly pick up birds afterwards, but although this is the traditional role of the breed, they can be just as much at home hunting out hedges and dense cover for the rough shooter. Their enthusiasm when working in water is legendary, and this, coupled with the thick coat which keeps a Labrador warm all day in the most severe weather, makes this breed the automatic choice of most wildfowlers. They

head. Its coat, which is long, straight and silky, is white with rich chestnut red markings. Welsh Springers have a friendly temperament, but are less busy and energetic than their English cousins, as well as being harder to train. They are also considerably more rarely seen in the shooting field.

The Sussex Spaniel, the Field Spaniel and the Clumber Spaniel are not often seen out shooting. However, each of these minor breeds has its small band of enthusiasts who breed, train and use them for their traditional shooting role, even if their real home these days is the show bench. The Sussex Spaniel is an old breed, long and low in build, and with a rich liver-coloured coat. It is slow in temperament and unlike other spaniels, may 'give tongue' when in pursuit of game.

The Field Spaniel originated through the interbreeding of the Springer and Sussex. Standing at around 45 cm, it is relatively short in the leg and long in the body. The Field Spaniel was originally very dark in colour but today has a flat, silky coat in rich shades of brown. Although relatively popular 50 years ago, it is rarely seen out shooting today.

Clumber spaniel

Working partner and faithful companion. This Labrador bitch has earned her keep on the grouse moor

may be either black or golden, which includes every hue from pale yellow to a sandy russet. Occasionally they are coloured a uniform chocolate brown.

Second in the popularity stakes amongst the retriever breeds is the Golden Retriever. Similar in size to the Labrador, the Golden Retriever has a longer coat, soft in texture and a rich golden yellow in colour. Formerly known as the Golden Flat-coat, it was bred originally from Flat-coated Retriever stock. The breed is very docile and affectionate, and its temperament has ideally suited it to the dual-purpose role of gundog and family pet. Golden Retrievers are reliable workers with good game-finding abilities, although they perhaps lack the flair of the Labrador. They are nevertheless quick learners and relatively easy to train.

In the early 1900s, the Flat-coated Retriever was probably the most frequently seen of all the retriever breeds in the shooting field, and was particularly popular amongst gamekeepers. It was not until after the First World War that the breed started to decline

and was eclipsed by the Labrador and the Golden Retriever. However, the Flat-coat still has its supporters, and indeed is now undergoing a revival in popularity. It has a longer, more aquiline head than either the Labrador or the Golden Retriever, and has a long, silky coat which is normally black, although brown dogs do occur. The Flat-coat is rather slow to mature, and so great patience is required in training.

Next amongst the retriever breeds are three dogs which are particularly noted for their distinctive waterproof coats. The Curly-coated Retriever, the Chesapeake Bay Retriever and the Irish Water Spaniel are all minor breeds in the retriever world, but they can occasionally be found out shooting, and probably have their strongest support amongst wildfowlers, who value their abilities as water dogs.

The Curly-coated Retriever is a big dog, standing between 65 and 70 cm high, with a distinctive short, dark, tight curly coat covering its body. Its head is large and powerful, and the facial hair is short and smooth. The Curly-coated Retriever is one of the oldest retriever breeds, and probably shares some ancestors with both the Labrador and the Poodle.

Originating in the eastern USA, the Chesapeake Bay Retriever is said to have been bred from two puppies rescued from a ship which ran aground off the coast of Maryland in 1807. Its brown coat, wavy rather than curly, is very dense and has an unusual oily texture which makes it extremely water resistant. This attribute makes the Chesapeake Bay Retriever particularly well adapted to working in cold, wet conditions. A strong swimmer, it is most popular amongst wildfowlers.

Golden retriever.

A team of Labradors at work after a grouse drive. The lab is the most popular of all the retrieving dogs.

Irish water spaniel.

Although sometimes classified with the spaniels, the Irish Water Spaniel is not a true spaniel at all. Coming from a long line of curly-coated water dogs, the present breed was established in Ireland in the 1850s by Mr Justice McCarthy. A big and extrovert dog, it is covered all over in curly ringlets of liver-coloured hair which is naturally oily and water-repellent. The tail, however, is smooth and tapers to a fine point. As their name implies, Irish Water Spaniels are most at home in rivers, fens and marshes – the wetter the better. Although they are slow to develop and take several years to mature, experienced Irish Water Spaniels are hard to beat when there are ducks or geese to be retrieved.

Pointing dogs

The pointers and setters are old-established breeds whose task it is to find game and indicate its whereabouts to the shooter. Before the days of large, organised shoots, when sportsmen using muzzle-loading guns hunted alone or in the company of one or two other shooters, shooting was a more leisurely activity than it sometimes is today. The need was for dogs which could 'quarter' or range back and forth across a grouse moor or the stubble fields of a partridge manor and, having located a covey of birds, ensure that they stayed where they were until the shooters arrived.

Pointing dogs, or bird dogs as they are often called in America, are therefore bred and trained to find game by means of its body scent. When working into the wind, so that the scent is blowing from the hidden game towards the dog, a good pointer or setter can detect birds or animals which are several metres away. It then stops and points towards the game, characteristically thrusting its muzzle forwards, raising a foreleg and levelling its tail, signalling to the guns to get into position for a shot. The dog should then remain perfectly still until instructed by its handler to flush the game. Working with pointing dogs is a complex business, and today it is mostly confined to the grouse moors of northern England and Scotland.

The English Pointer is the breed most often associated with pointing. It is a fine, elegant animal, smooth-coated and strong boned, and standing up to 70 cm tall. English Pointers are fast and active, often having to cover many miles of country as they range back and forth in front of the guns. Their scenting powers are extraordinarily well developed, and the deep muzzle and square-cut jowl lends the head an almost regal air. The neck is long and strong, built to keep that all-important nose questing as its owner travels at speed across the heather in search of game. English Pointers may be black and white or red and white, with the coloured markings often set against a mottled background coloration.

Setters are slightly smaller and more lightly built than English Pointers, with heads that are rather less square cut about the muzzle, although no less aristocratic in appearance. The most obvious difference, however, is that all the setter breeds are long-coated, with fine, silky hair and well-feathered tails. The English Setter was developed in the 1820s by Mr Edward Laverack, and for a while it was known as the Laverack Setter. It is predominantly white in colour, but mottled with grey or brown.

Gordon Setters, on the other hand are black and tan in colour, and are the only setters to have been developed in Scotland, where they were bred originally by the Dukes of Gordon. A workmanlike dog, the Gordon Setter is renowned for its stamina and perseverance. Although not as fast as the other setters, the Gordon is said to be particularly steady when on point.

The Irish Setter's ancestry is unknown, but can most likely be traced back to the spaniels, as the old Irish name of Red Spaniel indicates. In colour, Irish Setters may be anything from a golden chestnut to a deep mahogany red, and there are several working strains of dogs which are red and white in colour. The breed is noted for its keenness and endurance, although it is sometimes inclined to be headstrong and wilful. These days the Irish Setter is more likely to be seen on the show bench than in the shooting field.

Dogs which hunt, point and retrieve

There is one more category of gundogs to consider. These are the multi purpose or hunt-point-retrieve breeds – usually abbreviated to HPRs. Originating in continental Europe, the HPRs are versatile dogs, designed to find and point game, to flush it on command and then to retrieve it afterwards. They are at their best when working for just one or two shooters, and can make ideal all-purpose hunting dogs for the rough shooter who is prepared to put in the considerable time and effort needed for training.

Ranging out in front of the guns and running at speed through a field of roots or along a hedgerow, the HPR will, like the pointing breeds, detect the presence of game by its air scent. Ideally it should then point the bird or animal, allowing the shooter to get into position before being sent in to flush. Remaining steady as the shot is fired, the dog should then retrieve on command. Like spaniels, HPRs are expected to work in heavy cover, and most breeds normally have their tails docked to avoid getting the ends damaged.

It is fair to say that the average HPR will rarely carry out the individual hunting, pointing or retrieving tasks as well as the specialist spaniels, pointers and retrieving dogs, and there are several inherent vices that need careful watching, such as a tendency towards hard mouth in some breeds. In addition, the HPRs tend to be rather more individualistic and slow to mature than the more conventional gundogs. Nevertheless, a good HPR is a joy to shoot over, as an increasing number of shooters are starting to discover. Almost unknown in Britain before the 1950s, when they were 'discovered' by shooters serving in the British forces stationed in Germany, these multi-purpose dogs are now starting to receive the recognition they deserve amongst gundog enthusiasts in this country.

Some of the most popular HPR breeds were developed in Germany in the mid-1800s, and of these the German Shorthaired Pointer, or GSP, is the best known. It is a cross between the old German pointing dogs, the Bloodhound and the English Pointer, and is smooth-coated and mottled with a liver and white or black and white colouring, although some dogs can be almost completely black. The GSP is an intelligent and very active dog which needs plenty of exercise. It is a favourite amongst falconers and amongst woodland stalkers, who use it for tracking wounded deer.

Another mix of continental breeds, including the rough-coated Griffon hound and the German Shepherd dog, has produced the German Wirehaired Pointer, or GWP. Very

Flat-coated retriever.

English pointer.

popular in both Germany and Scandinavia, the GWP is fairly new to Britain. It is of a similar build to its short-haired cousin but has a rough, wiry protective coat flecked with liver and white, and a distinct 'beard' underneath its muzzle.

The Weimaraner is one of the oldest German pointing dogs, and dates from at least the mid-1600s. It is sleek, muscular and an unusual grey in colour. Weimaraners, which originated from the Weimar area of Germany, have good noses, and are obedient and friendly. Although the majority of dogs are smooth-coated, a long-haired variant does exist.

Amongst the German HPRs the Large Munsterlander is the least commonly encountered in Britain, although it is a beautiful dog to look at, with a setter-like head and a silky, long-haired coat in black and white, often with attractive mottling on the legs. The tail is well feathered.

From Hungary comes the Vizla, a rather smaller dog, although no less active in temperament than the GSP. Its smooth coat is golden russet in colour, and its ancestors include the ancient Transylvanian Hound and the Turkish Yellow Dog.

German wirehaired pointers. The HPR breeds are gaining rapidly in popularity.

German shorthaired pointer.

Hungarian vizla.

Weimaraner.

French crosses between local spaniel breeds and the English Setter produced the Brittany, sometimes still referred to as the Brittany Spaniel. This little dog, standing 45–52 cm high, has the busy temperament of its spaniel ancestors, and looks not unlike a long-legged spaniel. It has a long, soft coat marked with tan and white.

Finally, two Italian HPR breeds have recently been introduced to shooters in Britain. The Spinone is a very ancient breed, dating back to the 1200s, and related to the Griffon. Its long, wiry coat protects it when hunting in thick, thorny cover, but although it has a good nose, it is somewhat lacking in drive and perseverance. Nor is its retrieving capability all that it might be. The Bracco Italiano also takes life at a leisurely pace. A heavy-boned, smooth-coated dog, distinctively marked in red and white patches and flecks, it has a head which is strongly reminiscent of that of a Bloodhound. Although loyal, it is a slow-maturing dog with a tendency towards stubbornness.

Caring for a gundog

The decision to acquire a gundog is one of the most important that a shooter will make, and one from which a host of other choices will inevitably follow. Having decided which breed is most suitable, thought will have to be given to the dog's basic needs, such as kennelling, feeding and exercise. Veterinary care will have to be considered, and if it is decided to buy a young puppy, then it must be trained. All these questions are fundamental to establishing the all-important relationship between the shooter and his dog.

In many, if not most cases, the gundog is more than just a member of the team in the shooting field, it is part of the family. While the dog's 'job' may occupy it for a number of days throughout the shooting season, for the rest of the time it may well live the life of a family pet. There is nothing wrong with this, and there is no reason why a dog which spends the greater part of its life enjoying itself with a human family should not be a perfectly good shooting partner when the season comes round. Dogs quickly learn to recognise – and to enjoy – the task for which they are trained, and once in the field they will normally switch without any difficulty from the domestic to the working mode.

Housing

Even if it is to spend much of its time with the family, a dog which is expected to work does require managing in a rather different way from one which is wanted solely as a pet. For a start, a gundog should ideally be housed outside in a kennel. During the day, it may well spend its time in the house, in front of the fire or romping with young children, but at night it should be given its own quarters, with its own box or basket in which it can feel at home and where its own privacy will not be invaded by children or other pets. Ideally, these quarters should be in a purpose-built outdoor kennel with a run attached to it where the dog can enjoy a measure of freedom, fresh air and exercise. Alternatively an outhouse or shed will make good accommodation, as will a lobby area in the house.

A dog's night-time home should not be heated. Working gundog breeds are well able to withstand living outdoors even in the most severe winter weather, and if its days are spent soaking up the warmth of the kitchen radiator, night-time cold is the only thing which will ensure that it develops the thick, warm coat which will be necessary to protect it against rain, frost and brambles when it is out in the field. One only needs to compare a dog which lives in an outdoor kennel to one which stays in a heated kitchen at night to see how important the temperature of its living accommodation is to the development of its coat. Is it really fair to expect an animal which spends its entire life in a centrally heated house to work properly for a full, freezing day in the middle of January? Remember, while you can put on your thermal underwear and winter woollies if the thermometer dips below zero, your dog must make do with its own fur coat, whatever the weather.

Feeding and exercise

Feeding and exercise are two other considerations in which the needs of a working dog are very different from those of a full-time family pet. If you were to stay for weeks in front of the television in a heated living room, eating a diet of burgers, chips and chocolate cake, then you would not much like it if one day you were expected to pop outside and run a marathon or take part in a Premier League football match. In order to prepare yourself for any physical activity, you would want to keep yourself fit.

The same goes for a working dog. An overfed, overweight dog cannot possibly give of its best when out shooting or hunt eagerly and actively for a full, exhausting day in the field. It must be kept fit, at least during the shooting season. Fitness is simply a matter of establishing a balance between energy intake in the form of food, and energy expenditure in the form of muscle-building exercise. It is important, therefore, that feeding and exercise are both properly regulated routines, and that one is matched to the other. Of course every dog should have at least one, preferably two, daily walks, and while undergoing this level of exercise a standard feed regime can be established which maintains fitness. An active and enthusiastic temperament, a lean, muscular appearance and a glossy coat all tell of a dog's health and condition.

In the middle of the shooting season, when the dog is working regularly, the food intake can be increased. For example, after a hard day's work it is not unreasonable to give it twice or even three times its normal rations. Likewise, if the weather is cold and your dog is living outside, it will appreciate a modest increase in its rations to provide the extra energy it needs to keep warm.

Remember, however, that the recommendations given by most dog-food manufacturers are geared to a well-exercised animal which is fit and active, and that they are nothing more than a guide. Most medium-sized gundog breeds, such as the Labrador, will thrive on just two or three level mugfuls of a good-quality 'all-in-one' dry feed per day, soaked in warm water before it is given each evening. If the dog is looking thin, then step up the food. If it is starting to look fat, then reduce it. And remember also that any 'extras' such as titbits or kitchen scraps must be considered as part of the overall diet, and a dog which receives such things on a regular basis must have its normal feed reduced accordingly if it is to be kept fit and healthy.

Training a gundog puppy

Special thought must of course be given to the needs of a young puppy. There are few more exciting arrivals in the family home than that of a busy, lovable eight-week-old gundog puppy. In moments its natural energy and inquisitive temperament will have it diving into cupboards, pulling over waste bins and attacking the furniture. Such things come as second nature to puppies. From the first few days, however, you should try to establish the disciplined regime that will be part of its daily life when it becomes a grown-up gundog. Ensure that it is quickly house-trained if it is to live indoors, introduce it to its home in the kennel or outhouse and do not be surprised if it cries for the first few nights that it is on its own; in most cases this will quickly pass. Most importantly, establish those parts of the house in which it may live and those which are forbidden territory, making sure that young children know which rooms are out of bounds to the puppy so that they do not unfairly tempt it into them.

This understanding between both the older and the younger humans in the family and the puppy must continue throughout its life, and is no more crucial than when, at the age of six months or so, the time comes for it to start its training. At this critical stage, when the puppy is absorbing the lessons which will stay with it for years, it is absolutely vital that the messages given by the trainer are not undermined by other members of the family.

When it is being taught to walk to heel or to sit, for example, it must be emphasised to every member of the family, especially the younger ones, that the word 'sit' or 'heel', means just that. They are commands which must be obeyed, and not part of a great big game, the object of which is a rough-and-tumble on the lawn or in the living room. If every family member takes a hand in the training sessions, then they will all begin to see exactly how commands should be given and how they should be responded to by the dog.

As training becomes more advanced, this respect for the dog's developing working life becomes even more important, particularly with retrievers. A working retriever will have to sit quietly beside its handler, mark a falling bird and then, on command, use its eyes and nose or follow hand signals to locate the dead game. Finally, it must bring back the retrieve undamaged and deliver it promptly to the handler. How easy it is for all these lessons to be undermined by innocent and playful games such as the throwing of sticks when the dog is out for a family walk. In a few careless moments it learns that there is no need to wait for the command to retrieve, but that it is much more fun to gallop to where the stick is going to fall and then try to catch it as it does so. Then, as it chews at the stick on its way back, it realises that there is additional excitement to be had from a tug-of-war or a game of tag while the stupid human tries to grab the stick from its mouth.

In this way, a potentially brilliant retriever is taught to run-in to shot, to avoid promptly delivering game to hand while at the same time developing a 'hard mouth' which will damage game which it is sent to retrieve. The lesson is simple: never throw sticks for gundog puppies to pick up.

Few things are more lovable than a gundog puppy.

Retrieved to hand. A gundog is needed to find dead or wounded game.

Another lesson, however, can benefit greatly from family fun. A puppy is often wary of entering water, and there is no better way to overcome its natural caution than to have a jolly good romp with it in a shallow stream or pond, or even on the beach. Plenty of splashing and excitement soon makes it realise that water is really good fun and certainly nothing to be frightened of, and unlike practically every other aspect of gundog training, the introduction to water is a lesson in which the presence of an older dog is positively beneficial.

As the dog ceases to be a new arrival and starts becoming a member of the family, everyone can share in the tasks of feeding, exercising and grooming. Most dogs will revel in the attention they get, but no gundog will fail to recognise that the most important person is its master, its pack leader, the one who provides its sport and its purpose in life. Once the bond with its master is forged in the shooting field, a good, well-trained gundog of whatever breed will do anything it can to please.

THE MYSTERY OF SCENT

As every gundog owner will confirm, the ability of a dog to locate a quarry bird or animal varies from day to day, even from hour to hour. Although dogs' noses are many times more sensitive than our own, even their extraordinary scenting powers are controlled by factors such as temperature, moisture, wind, and ground conditions.

Scent will tend to be better when the ground temperature is low. A cold winter's day will be far better for the dogs than a mild and muggy one in early autumn, and very often scenting conditions will improve towards the end of a winter's afternoon as the temperature drops.

Damp conditions are better than dry ones because the beads of moisture on the vegetation seem to allow the scent to cling, making it easier for retrievers to hunt the line of a wounded bird. Too much moisture, on the other hand, is a disadvantage. Torrential rain will only wash out any scent that is present, making it much harder for dogs to work properly.

Wind is a very important factor for dogs which rely on body scent in order to locate game birds or animals. Spaniels, HPRs and pointing dogs should always be encouraged to work into the wind, so that the scent of the quarry is blown towards them. If the wind is strong, it makes the dogs' work very difficult, and they may very easily miss a bird which sits tight.

Different ground surfaces carry scent to varying degrees. Most retrievers will need to recover lost birds from thick cover where the scent is generally good. But if they have to follow a line over bare ground such as a ploughed field, then the lack of vegetation for the scent to cling to can make their job more difficult.

Labrador retriever. Dogs' noses are many times more sensitive than our own.

A well-dressed beater – Edwardian style.

CHAPTER 10
The Support Team

Although it may sound rather odd to say so, you do not need to have a gun in order to go out shooting. In fact there are many people who contribute to a day's shooting apart from the shooters, and many of them gain at least as much enjoyment and satisfaction from their contribution as the guns themselves. Among them are those who look after and manage the habitat in order to encourage a healthy population of game birds and animals, and those who rear and release game and protect it from predators. Then on a shooting day there are assistants such as beaters, stops and pickers-up, all of whom have important jobs to do, jobs which can make all the difference between the success and failure of the day's sport.

Some branches of shooting, of course, require little in the way of a supporting cast. Wildfowling and rough shooting are mostly solitary sports, without any of the complicated planning or organisation associated, for example, with driven pheasant shooting. But even so, wildfowlers often spend many hours in the summer months improving the wetland habitat and there is generally a warm welcome for anyone ready to help with planting trees or repairing bridges and access routes to the marsh, while there is always a need for volunteers to help with feeding flight ponds during the autumn and winter. Rough shooters also find that there is invariably plenty of work to do on the shoot throughout the year. They appreciate that the regular topping-up of game-feeding points in the woods will help to

ensure that there are birds about on shooting days, and many rough shooters even go so far as to release a few pheasants or partridges to augment the wild stock. However simple the rough shoot may be, there is generally something for willing hands to help with.

The gamekeeper

When it comes to the more organised forms of the sport, however, the key figure in shooting's support team is the gamekeeper. At one time, almost every estate had a head gamekeeper and often a team of several underkeepers to support him. Today there are probably only about 4,000 full-time professional gamekeepers in Britain. However, they are backed up by thousands more part-timers and amateur keepers who combine looking after the shoot with other paid jobs. Together this army of gamekeepers does an immense amount to maintain game stocks and to manage the countryside.

Game birds and animals are no different from any other forms of wildlife in that they require suitable habitats in which to flourish. One of the first tasks of the gamekeeper is therefore to ensure that the woods or moors are managed in such a way as to provide exactly the habitat needed. If the shoot is one where no reared game is released, then habitat conservation is even more important, for without it there will be little if anything for the guns to shoot at. Habitat management very often involves controlling the growth of vegetation. Pheasants, for example, are birds of the woodland edge, and do not like dark, gloomy forests. So the gamekeeper on a pheasant shoot may often have to spend time cutting rides or keeping the vegetation cleared from open pathways through the woods. The birds also prefer a wood which has a warm layer of undergrowth on the woodland floor to one which is cold and draughty. Encouraging this layer of undergrowth generally means letting more light through from the tree canopy by selective felling and the creation of open glades within the wood. Gamekeepers also like to see that any hedges around the outside of the wood are warm and windproof, in order to provide additional shelter for the birds.

The gamekeeper who is responsible for managing wild partridges will pay special attention to the hedgerows and field edges where the birds like to nest. He will try to ensure that the hedge itself is properly managed, with a broad, thick base to provide shelter, and that the grass alongside it is tall enough for partridges to nest in without being spotted by predators. Equally, he will want to see sufficient areas of short grass near to the nesting site, where the young chicks can dry themselves after heavy dew or rain. Without this the tiny birds may quickly chill and die.

On the grouse moor, habitat management

Vermin control is an important part of the gamekeeper's job.

For the hill keeper, fox control is essential.

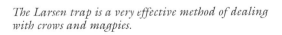

The Larsen trap is a very effective method of dealing with crows and magpies.

is a fundamental task. It is not commercially possible to rear and release grouse and therefore the only way of ensuring that they are plentiful is to create the right habitat for wild birds to breed and successfully bring up large numbers of young chicks. This is done by burning small strips or patches of heather in the early spring. After the moor has been burned, new heather shoots very quickly sprout again to form a succulent carpet of young growth on which the birds can feed, and within a few years, the young heather will grow up to form a thick, protective canopy within which the birds can nest in security. When it has become old and straggly, the heather is burned once again. So heather burning, when carried out in rotation, creates a diverse and varied habitat, with areas of young growth interspersed with older heather to create exactly the conditions which grouse need.

In addition to a suitable habitat, game birds and animals need security and freedom from predation if they are to thrive and multiply. If the gamekeeper can ensure that the game population contains a shootable surplus, then it will be possible during the season for a harvest of game to be taken without endangering the long-term future of the species. However, if that surplus ends up in the jaws of stoats and the stomachs of foxes, or if its nests are raided by crows and magpies, then no matter how hard he tries, there will be little for the guns to see or shoot at when the shooting season comes round.

The most important ground predators of game are foxes, stoats and rats, while feral mink can do great damage to game and wildfowl near water where the mink live. Gamekeepers control foxes with snares, by digging them out of their earths with terriers and by shooting them, generally with a rifle. In districts regularly hunted by foxhounds, the hunt can also play a useful part in fox control and on estates where both hunting and shooting take place, the keeper will normally try to strike a balance between ensuring that there are sufficient foxes for the hounds to find when they come in the winter, and ensuring that there are not so many that all his pheasants get eaten. A code of practice published by the BASC advises on the correct use of snares for catching foxes.

Stoats, mink and other small predators are normally caught in tunnel traps. These consist of approved spring traps such as Fenn traps, which are placed in small, specially constructed tunnels. Inquisitive ground predators entering the tunnel are quickly caught. Other small ground vermin such as rats and mice may be trapped with conventional break-back traps. Cage traps are also extensively used for pest control. These are often baited with food, and animals entering them are caught alive and dispatched later by the gamekeeper. By law, all traps and snares must be inspected every day. Rats and mice may also be controlled with poison. However, there are very strict rules about how poison may be used in the countryside, to avoid its being taken by non-target species.

Winged predators such as the carrion crow and the magpie do very serious damage at nesting time by plundering the eggs of pheasants, partridges and many other wild birds. They have to be controlled, and this is normally done either by shooting or with cage traps. A particularly popular and effective cage trap is the Larsen trap, invented by a Danish gamekeeper. It consists of two compartments, into one of which is placed a live decoy bird. This entices wild birds down to the other compartment, which is fitted with a spring-loaded trap door. Once caught, the trapped bird is removed and destroyed. Larsen traps have been very effective in checking the rapid spread of magpies into some parts of the countryside.

Another form of predator which the gamekeeper has to guard against is the two-legged variety – the poacher. The romantic image of the old village poacher taking 'one for the pot' is a thing of the past. Most poaching is carried out by gangs, who may take large

This fox snare is being set outside a release pen. Note the electric wire which is being used to provide the young pheasant poults in the pen with extra protection from foxes.

amounts of game before escaping quickly and offering it for sale to pubs, restaurants and unscrupulous dealers. Deer poachers often use particularly cruel methods which do not quickly kill the animal, such as snares, crossbows or low-powered rifles, and as a result they cause great suffering. Other poachers use lurchers to course and kill hares and rabbits, and if challenged by the farmer, landowner or gamekeeper, they will turn violent. Many gamekeepers operate effective security systems on their shoots to suppress poaching, and have close working relationships with the local police.

On many shoots, pheasants, partridges and sometimes ducks are reared and released to supplement the wild stock, and where this takes place it is the gamekeeper's responsibility to manage the rearing and releasing programme. This will often entail a great deal of work and very long hours, especially at busy times of the year such as when the eggs are hatching and when the young poults are first released into the woods.

This keeper is feeding the pheasants in his laying pen.

Some gamekeepers carry out the entire incubation and rearing process on their employers' estates, and this means that they have to start with large numbers of eggs. These can either be bought from a specialist game farm or collected from hen pheasants which have been caught up at the end of the shooting season and put, together with a number of cock pheasants, into a large open laying pen. The eggs then have to be incubated. Traditionally this was done by large numbers of broody chickens which acted as foster-mothers to the young game bird chicks, and if only a few birds need to be reared, then broodies are sometimes still used. Nowadays, however, most estates employ a mechanical incubator which can accommodate a large number of eggs at a time and keep them at a constant temperature until it is time for them to hatch. The young chicks are then reared to the age of six or eight weeks, when they are introduced into the wild. If the estate does not wish to undertake the entire incubation and rearing process itself, the gamekeeper may obtain day-old pheasant chicks or six-week-old poults from a game farm.

A basket full of pheasant eggs ready for incubation, collected from the laying pen

Small quantities of game, like these partridges, may be reared under broody hens.

Day-old pheasant chicks straight out of the incubator.

Topping up the feed hopper in a release pen. There are always plenty of jobs to do on the shoot.

When they are first released into the woods, pheasant poults are put into a release pen. This is a large, open-topped pen which is normally situated in a wood, and which encloses natural cover such as trees and bushes in order that the poults can learn to fend for themselves. The sides are about 3 metres high, and are made of wire netting which can be let into the ground in order to prevent foxes from digging their way in. Sometimes a low electric fence is placed around the outside for added protection against foxes. At strategic points around it there are pop holes in the wire through which, in due course, the birds may come and go. Water and food, normally whole grain, are supplied every day by the gamekeeper, and as they gradually get accustomed to their new surroundings, the birds will be allowed out through the pop holes to explore the wood adjacent to the pen. By the beginning of the shooting season, the pheasants will be fully developed, flying strongly and completely accustomed to life in the wild. At this stage the release pen will be permanently open and the birds will be able to come and go as they please, the gamekeeper keeping them in the woods only by means of regular feeding.

Partridges are normally released not in woods but in specially established game-cover crops out in the fields, while mallard are released onto a suitable lake or pond. Like pheasants, both partridges and mallard require constant attention to prevent them from straying in search of food.

With habitat management, predator control and game rearing to keep him occupied, the gamekeeper is busy in all seasons. Very often he will be glad of some extra help, and one of the very best ways in which to learn about how a shoot works is to offer to spend a few hours assisting him with tasks such as building and repairing release pens or carrying food and water for the birds. If you are lucky, you will begin to learn about the rearing and management of game and the skill

and the fieldcraft involved in such activities as trapping and predator control. More than that, you will soon start to appreciate and understand the lives and habits of the other wild creatures which live on or around the shoot.

Beaters

One occasion when help is always needed is on a formal shooting day, when a range of assistants is required to ensure that everything goes smoothly. Beaters, stops, and pickers-up may all be needed, and the non-shooter can help with these tasks, learning much in the process and getting a great deal of pleasure out of a day in the countryside.

The beater's job is to drive game towards the guns, and although the task may sound simple, there is in fact considerable skill involved in beating, which makes it an enjoyable and interesting job as well as an energetic one. Beaters, or brushers as they are sometimes called, work as a team, under the supervision of a gamekeeper or head beater, and if you are spending a day beating, the first rule to remember is that any instructions which you are given must be followed exactly. If you stray out of line or decide to go to a different part of the wood from that to which you were sent, then you could well find yourself in danger from stray shots from guns who do not realise that you are there. Generally the instructions to the beaters will be given by a blast on a whistle. Make sure that you know what the signals mean, and if an instruction is given to halt a drive, then stop immediately and do not move forward again until you are told to.

Do not try to rush through the cover, for if you do so you will almost certainly pass over birds which are sitting tight, and furthermore you will make it difficult for the other beaters to keep in a straight line with you. Remember that it is your job to put the birds over the guns one by one in a steady stream, not to force them over in a single mad rush. The reason for this is that if all the birds flush together, then instead of being able to shoot at a sensible pace throughout the drive, the guns will stand idle for much of the time and then spend a few moments frantically trying to reload as a rapid succession of birds flies over their heads. As a beater, you will therefore need to watch closely for birds moving in front of you. If you see several which look as though they are all about to flush at once, stand still and tap steadily with your stick until they flush one by one or until they move forward into the next patch of cover.

If you have a dog, you can get enormous fun from working it in the beating line. There is no doubt that the presence of a few good dogs, spaniels in particular, make all the difference to the success of a drive. The dogs will find and push up game that you never knew was there, producing many more birds for the guns to shoot at. However, your dog must be well trained, and must not be allowed to rush ahead, chasing game and flushing it in a wild and uncontrolled manner. Carry a slip-lead with you – a gundog should never wear a conventional collar when it is working in case it gets caught by brambles or barbed wire – and if your dog is becoming over-excited put it on the lead for a while until it has calmed down again.

A dog is very useful for getting into the really tough pieces of cover that you will often find in the middle of a wood. However, if you do not have a dog with you, then you will have to try and bash through these places yourself, no matter how forbidding they may seem. If you do not, then you can be quite sure that is where all the birds will be and if you skirt round the outside you will miss them. Conversely, if you are working through a block of game-cover crop like maize or arti-chokes, then make sure that someone walks around the outside, tapping with a stick as he goes. If the outside of the cover is not guarded in this way, then the birds will quickly take advantage of the situation by

A beater and his spaniel. The presence of a few good dogs in the beating line makes all the difference to the success of a drive.

running back to safety around the perimeter of the cover crop, unseen by the beaters who are energetically bashing their way through the middle.

The keeper and his team of beaters. An essential part of the game shooting scene.

Beaters can lend a hand by carrying game back to the game cart at the end of a drive.

Another question to consider when beating is the extent to which you should use your voice. As a general rule, the wilder the birds, the less noise you should make. On a genuine wild bird shoot, the pheasants or partridges will run or flush the moment they hear the slightest noise, and all that is required is a steady tap, tap, tapping with your stick as you move forward. It is a real delight to watch an experienced team of beaters at work with wild game. Where reared birds are present, a little more verbal encouragement may be used, but even then, nobody wants to hear shouting and yelling, and the best way of encouraging birds to move and flush in a controlled manner is still to tap with your stick.

When beating on a walked-up shoot, you may well be walking alongside the guns. If so, and particularly if you have a dog with you, lend a hand by carrying any shot game back to the game cart or to the place where it is collected at the end of the drive.

If you are going out for a day's beating, then make sure that you dress sensibly, for you will almost certainly have to go through thick, possibly wet cover. A waxproof coat is best, and thornproof overtrousers or leggings will be an enormous help and will stop your legs from being scratched. Wellington boots are ideal for most situations. However, if you are invited to beat on a grouse moor on a hot August day, you may well find that a pair of jeans and a T-shirt are all that you need. But do remember to wear stout ankle boots and perhaps a pair of gaiters, for heather is very abrasive around your ankles. As for equipment, the only thing you will need is a good stout stick.

Beating is open to both sexes and all ages, and most shoots are constantly on the look-out for good, reliable beaters. Of course it helps if you already know the local game-keeper, for it is his responsibility to recruit the beating team, but a few words with one of his regular beaters should soon gain you an intro-duction. If you have been beating regularly on a shoot throughout the winter, you may well find yourself asked to the keeper's day at the end of the season, when the gamekeeper has the chance of inviting all those who have helped him during the course of the year for a day's shooting.

Flags are useful for turning birds back towards the guns.

Stops

A particularly important member of the beating team is the stop. His job is to prevent game from leaking out of the side of the drive at a vulnerable point. A wood which forms the main part of a drive may, for example, have a ditch or hedgerow leading off it and connecting it with a neighbouring piece of cover. This escape route will be well known to all the game birds which live in the vicinity, and will be used as a natural corridor or pathway. When a line of beaters comes through the wood, the birds will naturally make a beeline for it. The result will be that instead of flushing and flying forward over the guns, they will run as quickly as possible along the ditch and disappear out of the drive, unless they are prevented from doing so by a stop.

The stop taps quietly with his stick to prevent game from 'leaking' out of the drive.

If you are asked to act as stop, you should take up position at the start of the drive, standing at the point where the ditch or hedge leaves the main wood, so blocking the exit route for any game. Remember that your objective should be to head the birds back into the wood rather than to put them up into the air. From the moment the drive starts, you should tap quietly with your stick, watching closely for any birds which run towards you. You will often spot a steady procession of pheasants heading through the undergrowth in your direction, only to see them turn back into the wood the moment that they realise you are there.

Do not shout or make a lot of noise; there is no need to do so. All that is required is a steady tapping, as this is without doubt the most effective way of ensuring that the birds go in the intended direction, over the guns.

Flag men

Sometimes a number of beaters will be given flags, normally made from plastic fertiliser bags attached to sticks. These are used to turn game birds, such as partridges and grouse, and can be very effective when game is being driven from open country, such as a field of roots or a grouse moor. A covey of birds which gets up will very often fly along the line of beaters rather than away from it, and if it is not quickly turned, then it will almost certainly escape out of the side of the drive. That is what the flag men are there to prevent.

If you are given a flag, you may well be asked to walk in a strategic part of the beating line, such as on a flank or ridge over which the birds might be tempted to fly. If you see any birds heading towards you, wave your flag in an effort to turn them forwards and towards the guns. Remember that flags are most effective when sparingly used. A well-timed wave at the critical moment will be far more effective at turning a fast-flying covey of partridges than a continual half-hearted flap.

Pickers-up

Situated behind the guns on a driven shoot are some very important members of the support team. Without the pickers-up and their dogs, a very large proportion of the shot game would probably never be recovered. While the birds which fall close to the guns' feet can usually be picked up with relative ease, those which drop several hundred metres behind the line, as well as wounded birds which have sufficient strength to reach a distant piece of cover, have to be carefully marked and then quickly collected by a retrieving dog.

The pickers-up and their dogs will watch each bird closely as it flies over the guns. They will note those that are shot at and, even if they do not fall, they will watch for tell-tale signs that they have been hit by just one or two pellets. The bird might flinch in mid-air or a leg might drop as the shot is fired. If so, a dog will be sent to find it once it has landed. Wounded birds such as these, together with those which drop well behind the line, will often be picked up while the drive is in progress. Those that have fallen close to the guns will be collected when it has finished. Each picker-up will probably have a team of two, three or even four superbly trained dogs, so that the pick-up can be completed quickly and efficiently.

It is considered a great honour to be invited to pick up at a big shoot, and only when you have one or more very well-trained dogs which are absolutely steady and reliable, and probably several years of experience in the shooting field yourself, are you likely to be invited to go picking up. Meanwhile, if you get the chance, do try to watch an experienced picker-up in action. To do so is to see gundog work at its best.

Dispatching game

A further task with which pickers-up, beaters,

and indeed all who shoot must be familiar is the humane dispatch of wounded game. No shooter likes to wound the animals or birds he shoots, and a quick, clean kill must always be the ultimate objective whenever the trigger is pulled. However, an instant kill is an ideal which is not always achieved, and the gundogs will occasionally bring back a wounded bird which has to be killed right away. The best and most humane way of doing so is with a short weighted stick or 'priest', often with a head made of stag's horn filled with lead. Holding the bird in one hand with its head and neck extended, you should smartly strike the back of the head with the priest. If this procedure is correctly carried out, then a single blow will be all that is required to kill it.

A rabbit or hare requires a different technique. Experienced vermin controllers are able, with a quick movement of the hand, to dislocate the neck vertebrae, and this is perhaps the quickest and most effective way of dispatching furred game. A very effective alternative, however, is to hold the animal up by its hind legs with one hand, and then strike the back of its neck sharply and firmly with the side of the other hand, just behind the ears. This should break the neck instantly.

All dispatching of game should be done quickly and discreetly, using methods which cause the least damage to the carcass. Do not, therefore, adopt the frequently-used technique of holding a pheasant by the head and swinging its body round in a circle. If you are skilled, you may break the neck quickly. If you are not, then you are more likely to remove the head from the body. Finally, try to avoid dispatching wounded birds or animals in front of passers-by, as your actions might be misinterpreted or give offence.

A picker-up and his team of three willing helpers.

The keeper collects the game at the end of the drive.

Once it is safely in the game larder, the game is carefully hung up to await collection by the game dealer.

Hedge laying in Leicestershire, sponsored by the hunt. Field sports have provided the incentive to retain and manage traditional landscape features.

CHAPTER 11

Shooting and the Countryside

Although the woods, moors and marshes of Britain may look natural enough, they are in fact part of a rural landscape which is almost entirely artificial. Since the time when successive waves of immigrant peoples – Neolithic, Bronze Age and Iron Age – first cleared the virgin forests in order to create farmland, the face of our countryside has been shaped by man. On a framework of hills, valleys, rivers and mountains supplied by mother nature, he has over 10,000 years crafted a covering, a minutely detailed mantle which, if studied with care and understanding, will reveal all manner of hidden secrets about its history and development.

An old earthwork, a hedgerow, the curved boundary of an ancient woodland or the broad grass verges beside a country road all tell us something about the people who created the rural landscape, and the economic and social pressures which made them dig, build, plant and hew. The activities which have done most to shape the British countryside are, not surprisingly, farming and forestry, for the production of food and timber have always utilised large tracts of land and continue to do so today. Close behind them, however, come field sports, and you do not have to look far to see the impact which hunting has made on the landscape. The reason that areas like the New Forest in Hampshire, Ashdown Forest in Sussex or Wychwood Forest in Oxfordshire remain wild and wooded is because long ago the Norman kings designated them as hunting areas and

forbade their destruction or cultivation.

Some of the spirit of these royal hunting reserves was later embodied in the estates of great landowners who created their own deer parks and who, from the late 1700s onwards, planted many small woodlands in order to make the countryside more suitable for the increasingly popular sport of foxhunting. In the late 1800s, however, the rise of game shooting as an important economic activity and a central focus for the social structure of the countryside led to the complete redesigning of shooting estates and the planting of vast numbers of new woods, coverts and shelter belts, many of which still exist today. In a very real sense, shooting has helped shape the fabric of the countryside, and as we shall see, it still exerts a great influence over the management of the land, an influence which has helped to counterbalance some of the more extreme demands made by commercial farming.

Shooting and the farmed landscape

For a period of around 120 years up to the Second World War, the British countryside changed very little. The landscape of small fields enclosed by hedges, banks or stone walls supported systems of mixed farming in which the raising of livestock and the growing of crops went hand in hand. However, wartime food shortages led to a complete reorganisation of agriculture, which was

More wheat but less wildlife habitat. Farm intensification has led to the loss of hedgerows, trees and woodlands.

modernised and mechanised throughout the 1950s and 1960s in an attempt to make Britain self-sufficient in the food which her climate would allow her to produce. When in 1973 this country joined the European Community and became subject to the Common Agricultural Policy, the process of agricultural mechanisation and intensification gathered speed. Many miles of hedgerow were removed to create larger fields, old pastures were drained and turned over to cereal growing, and marginal land was brought under the plough. The changes to the countryside and its wildlife were very rapid indeed, and people now accept that many of them were damaging.

Landowners with traditional shooting estates, however, often resisted the financial pressures which encouraged more intensive farming. They knew that the loss of hedges and woodlands would damage or destroy the habitat for game birds. Even in places like East Anglia, where the changes in farming practice were at their most sweeping, farms and estates where the owners have an interest in shooting have retained their traditional landscape features such as hedgerows, woodlands and copses. Shooting has therefore helped to preserve the countryside.

This new farm woodland was planted by a shooting landowner to provide cover for game birds.

BELOW:
Where shooting takes place, farmers are often more sympathetic towards the landscape and wildlife habitats.

ABOVE:
Reduction in the use of pesticides has allowed many wild flowers to reappear on arable farmland.

In addition, shooting and game conservation also provide an important incentive for farmers and landowners to manage the land more sympathetically. They see that if the habitat for game is improved, they and their friends derive more enjoyment from shooting over their farms, or they can let the shooting rights in order to obtain extra income. In addition, they know that long-term improvements such as the creation of new woodlands and game coverts will improve the capital value of their farms. These more sympathetic approaches to countryside management have been strongly promoted by organisations like the Game Conservancy Trust.

Farmers with an interest in shooting have been among the first to create conservation headlands, 6 metre wide strips around the edges of cereal fields in which the use of pesticide sprays is greatly restricted. Because many broad-leaved weeds are able to survive in these conservation headlands, the population of insects which live on them is much higher than it is in the rest of the field. The insects in turn provide food for young game bird chicks and many other bird species besides, contributing greatly to a more diverse bird population.

The improvement of farms for shooting has encouraged the planting of many thousands of hectares of new farm woodlands, which generally incorporate native tree species such as oak, chestnut, wild cherry, alder and beech. They are often carefully designed so as to take advantage of the natural topography of the land for shooting purposes, and to create the best possible distribution of game cover on the farm. As they grow and mature they will become important features in the landscape, replacing at least some of the farmland trees which were removed in the years between 1960 and 1985.

Those farmers with a particular interest in shooting have in many cases managed and conserved their hedges, or planted new ones. The reason for this is that hedges are important for game. The banks on which they grow provide nesting sites for pheasants and, more especially, partridges. The hedges themselves provide shelter and form corridors along which game may move around the farm. And on shooting days they are used to drive game over in order to provide more exciting sport. Likewise, farm ponds are often to be found on shooting estates, where they have been retained or newly created in order to provide habitats for species such as mallard and snipe.

Game conservationists have also had an important part to play in making the Government's farming policies more environmentally friendly. When set-aside was first introduced in order to take farmland out of cereal production, farmers were forced by law to mow or cultivate their set-aside land in early summer – just at the time when ground-nesting birds were raising their young. The destruction of game birds and other wildlife by ploughs and mowing machines was immense, and the outcry against it was led by bodies such as the Game Conservancy Trust. Thanks in part to the strong pressure from shooting farmers, the set-aside rules were changed so as to avoid the need to mow or cultivate during the nesting season, and set-aside land now forms a valuable refuge and larder for many species of wildlife from harvest time right through to the following summer.

The more environmentally sensitive farming practices which shooting has encouraged have not only boosted game birds, however. A whole host of other species of birds, animals, plants and insects has also benefited. Wild flowers like the poppy, ox-eye daisy and cornflower have returned in profusion to the conservation headlands of cereal fields, bringing with them a significant increase in the numbers of hedgerow butterflies. Improvements to the set-aside rules have aided small ground-nesting birds like the skylark, while it seems that the brown hare is also enjoying the more diversified habitat which set-aside has created. Farmers and landowners with an interest in shooting have promoted the 'greening' of agriculture, and continue to provide a strong environmental input into government thinking on country-side matters.

Woodlands

Woodlands and field sports have had a long association. As the Ice Age glaciers retreated and Britain finally became separated from continental Europe, the country was cloaked in a single great forest, consisting of hazel, elm, oak, alder, small-leaved lime and a number of other species. Over the succeeding millennia, Neolithic, Bronze Age and Celtic peoples gradually cleared large areas of forest to create land in which to farm and build their villages, but the wildwood on the edge of the fields and settled areas remained a place where they could hunt game, and soon assumed further economic importance as a source of fuel, timber, building materials, grazing and animal food. Formal protection of woodlands was given as long ago as 1184, when the Assize of Woodstock preserved forests as royal hunting grounds, and succeeding Norman and Plantagenet kings enlarged and expanded the network of royal forests and private hunting reserves or chases. Strict laws were enacted to protect the environment of the deer which roamed the forest, which successive monarchs and their nobles enjoyed hunting. These laws prevented the cutting down of trees and the grubbing-up or 'assarting' of woodland to create new farm-land. Forest wardens and foresters were made responsible for apprehending poachers and looking after the deer, and heavy penalties were exacted from offenders. Although the royal forests contained large areas of open ground and were not by any means entirely wooded, the protection given to them in the Middle Ages ensured the survival of important wooded landscapes all over Britain.

Down the centuries, landowners have continued to plant and protect woodland for the purpose of sport, and in the nineteenth century the development of the great shooting estates saw the planting of extensive new woods as cover for pheasants. Despite the ravages of two world wars, which saw much felling of valuable timber, many of these woods still exist today, and sportsmen continue to protect woods because of their value for game.

They also continue to plant new woods. A recent survey of farmers and estate owners demonstrated the close link between shooting and the presence on estates of significant areas of woodland. On the 1,400 farms and estates which were investigated, 96 per cent of woodland was found on shooting estates, and half the non-shooting estates which were surveyed had no woodland at all. The more large-scale the shooting, the more likely there was to be woodland managed for game. Shooting owners were found to be more active not only in conserving existing woodlands, but also in planting new ones. While 61 per cent of landholders releasing game birds for shooting had planted new woodlands, only 21 per cent of those not releasing game had done so.

Woods must be managed as well as being planted and protected, and shooting sportsmen have an excellent record in woodland management. Pheasants are birds of the woodland edge, and prefer an open wooded habitat with plenty of glades where sunlight can reach the woodland floor. This has encouraged sporting landowners to revive the old practice of coppicing, a form of woodland management in which trees are cut down to ground level and then allowed to regrow from the stumps or 'stools'. Traditionally, coppicing was carried out to provide timber for fuel, building, thatching, hurdlemaking and furniture making. Today it is just as frequently undertaken to produce ideal habitat for game, and shooting owners are seven times more likely to have coppiced their woodlands than non shooting owners. They are also four times more likely to have planted

Wychwood Forest was first preserved for hunting 800 years ago. Today it is managed as part of a sporting estate.

shrubs around their woodlands as windbreaks or to provide warmth and security for game birds.

Shoot management also involves creating and maintaining rides through the woods on which standing guns can be positioned on shooting days, and opening 'skylights' in the woodland canopy in order that pheasants may be flushed out of the woods to present high, fast-flying shots to the guns below. Woodland management prescriptions are carefully detailed by organisations like the Game Conservancy Trust, in order that owners and foresters may combine the best possible game shooting with their other woodland enterprises such as timber production.

Where woodlands are well looked after, a wide range of wildlife species benefits. Sporting woodlands are home to several rare woodland butterflies such as the Duke of Burgundy fritillary and the purple emperor. Where coppicing is undertaken, wild flowers such as bluebells, primroses, violets and wood anemones thrive and bloom, as do many species of wild fungus. Woodland birds appreciate the diverse and well-managed habitat which shooting creates, and benefit from the protection to their eggs and young which is provided by the control, by gamekeepers, of winged predators like crows, magpies and jays. Sporting woodlands are frequently noted for the variety of birdsong which can be heard in them during spring.

Woodlands are also home to the six species of deer which are found in Britain, and while

A well-managed woodland ride on a shooting estate.
Many woods only exist because of their sporting value.

Shooting owners have revived the old practice of
coppicing.

their presence often complements the conservation of game and wildlife, they are not always welcome to the forester because of the damage they can do to the growing shoots and the bark of young trees. Sporting management will therefore often included the control of deer at acceptable levels. Properly regulated woodland stalking ensures a healthy deer population with the right balance of young and old, and of male and female animals, whilst it can also yield a valuable extra income to the woodland owner in the form of stalking fees from visiting sportsmen.

Wetlands

Wetlands are some of the most threatened of Britain's semi-natural habitats. For thousands of years, people have prized level sites along the flood plains of rivers or close to the edges of tidal estuaries for building their villages, towns, cities and ports, while the rich, deep alluvial soils of our river valleys have proved some of the most fertile for farming. As a result, only a tiny proportion of this country's once extensive marshes and wetlands remain in anything approaching their natural state. Yet these places remain a vital habitat for hundreds of thousands of wildfowl and wading birds which migrate here in autumn and winter from the far north, and we therefore have an international responsibility to conserve and protect them.

Bird conservation bodies have done a great deal by buying and managing important reserve areas, but wildfowlers have also been a major force in wetland conservation. Since 1908, when the Wildfowlers Association of Great Britain and Ireland (WAGBI) was formed, wildfowlers have recognised that unless wetlands are protected, ducks and geese will disappear and with them the sport of wildfowling. The principles of habitat conservation are today embodied in WAGBI's successor, the BASC, and around the country its 220 affiliated wildfowling clubs manage 105,000 hectares of marsh and wetland, over 90 per cent of which is officially designated as Sites of Special Scientific Interest because of its very high nature-conservation value.

Wildfowlers undertake practical conservation activities, such as wardening sites, creating and maintaining access routes across marshes, clearing litter, planting trees, managing ponds and water levels, cutting and managing vegetation and controlling pests. These activities are very often undertaken on behalf of voluntary conservation bodies such as county wildlife trusts, or the Government's own nature conservation agencies. Wild-fowlers also look after nature reserves situated within the sites where they shoot. For example, one club manages an important spring breeding site for terns on the nature reserve where its members shoot during the winter.

Many landowners with an interest in wildfowling own important wetland sites, and wildfowling clubs are increasingly buying other similar sites as they come up for sale. A valuable source of funds for land purchase is the BASC's Wildlife Habitat Trust, which raises money for conservation from within the shooting community. Thus very large areas of wetland, both around the coast and inland, are under the direct control of shooting owners who manage them in accordance with the best principles of conservation.

Because wildfowlers have a vested interest in the conservation of wildfowl habitats, they are also among the first to protest against plans to develop or destroy valuable wetland sites. These plans are frequently put forward by commerce or industry, and wildfowlers have contributed to successful campaigns against the building of destructive tidal barrages across our estuaries. Moreover, together with other traditional estuary users, they also add their voice to protests against further damaging developments like the building of marinas and industrial estates. In addition, wildfowlers closely monitor pollution, and are often the first to alert the conservation authorities to accidents such as oil spillages.

Their responsible work for conservation has earned wildfowlers the respect of many conservation bodies, and today they take their place alongside other interest groups whenever the planning or management of estuaries, coastal zones and other major wetland sites is discussed.

Moorlands

One of the most important types of landscape

in northern and western Britain is moorland. The wide, open hills of the uplands, purple with heather in the summer and bleak and forbidding in winter, are highly valued for their scenic beauty and are also home to a unique range of wildlife. Indeed, some moorland species are found only in the British Isles. Heather moors, however, are in decline. In the past 30 years, the area of heather moorland in England and Scotland has shrunk by around 20 per cent, and up to 70 per cent of what remains is at risk. Conversion to agricultural land was once the principal reason for the disappearance of moorland, but today the main threats come from forestry and from overgrazing by sheep and, increasingly, deer.

Wetlands are some of our most threatened habitats.

Ponds and lakes, such as this one in Oxfordshire, are protected and preserved by sporting estate owners.

Wet meadows are a vital habitat for migratory birds.

This salt marsh in Essex was bought by a wildfowling club with help from the Wildlife Habitat Trust, which raises money for conservation from the shooting community.

However, heather moors also have an important economic value, for they are home to that most prized of all game birds, the red grouse. Nearly half a million hectares of moorland is used for grouse shooting, representing a third of the entire moorland area of Britain. Where grouse are plentiful, the financial rewards to the moorland owners are able to cover the high cost of continued traditional management of the heather by rotational burning. As we have seen, gamekeepers burn the heather in order to create a patchwork of different-aged growth which enables a pair of grouse to rear a large brood of healthy chicks in a relatively small breeding territory. This is why a well-managed moor supports the highest concentration of grouse. Management of heather for grouse deliberately sets out to create a particularly rich and diverse habitat, and this in turn benefits a host of other species such as the golden plover, greenshank and merlin, all of which form part of the moorland wildlife community. Thus a valuable conservation asset is maintained and managed, thanks to shooting.

Where there are insufficient grouse to warrant shooting, perhaps because of heavy predation by foxes or winged predators, or because overgrazing has destroyed the patchwork of mixed-aged heather which red grouse need, the estate may be unable to justify paying for a gamekeeper to undertake the necessary intensive heather management and predator control, and the moor will go into further decline. If it remains economic to use the land for grazing sheep, then at least the moor stands a chance of survival, even though its biodiversity is considerably reduced. However, should even sheep farming become unprofitable, then the only option which remains is for the moor to be planted with trees, at which point the traditional habitat and its wildlife will be lost. Moreover, the populations of predators like foxes which multiply rapidly in the new conifer forests will threaten the survival of grouse in those areas of heather moorland which remain alongside them.

Throughout the moorlands of Scotland and northern England, grouse shooting therefore has a fundamental role in preserving a unique landscape and wildlife resource, a fact which is well recognised by many of the conservation organisations and agencies. They appreciate that it would simply not be possible for the Government alone to cover the costs of moorland management, and that it is often only grouse shooting which is saving these important landscapes from destruction. In the case of the heather moor, shooting may be nothing less than a lifeline upon which the survival of the habitat depends.

Conclusion

Shooting and nature conservation are inextricably linked; indeed they are dependent upon one another. It is self-evident that unless quarry populations are conserved by the activities of people like gamekeepers and other land managers, shooting could not possibly exist. What is less obvious, however, is that a great deal of nature conservation actually depends on shooting. Only a tiny proportion – around 2 per cent – of the land surface of Britain is covered by nature reserves, in which official policy and resources work for the survival of wild species. The vast majority of the countryside – some 88 per cent – is managed by farmers and land-owners, and about half of this sustains some form of shooting. Whether it be on moorland or marsh, farmland or forest, shooting management improves the habitat for an enormous variety of plant and animal species, far beyond the relatively small number of game birds and mammals for which sportsmen have a direct and primary concern. The income which shooting provides, and the interest in conservation which it sustains amongst land managers creates an incentive for the protection and care of the countryside, providing a bulwark against the worst

Wildfowlers undertake important conservation management work, like building bridges and maintaining access routes across the marshes.

excesses of intensive farming and forestry.

Without the income and the enthusiasm for voluntary conservation which shooting generates, it is hard to see how government-funded conservation, provided at the taxpayer's expense, could cope. Without shooting, the countryside would most certainly be the poorer.

This Essex marsh is owned and managed by a wildfowling club as part of a National Nature Reserve.

Moorland management for grouse shooting produces a varied patchwork of habitats which are rich in wildlife.

The Shooting Organisations

The British Association for Shooting and Conservation

Marford Mill
Rossett
Wrexham
LL12 0HL
Tel: 01244 573000
Fax: 01244 573001
Email: enq@basc.org.uk
Web: www.basc.org.uk

Countryside Alliance

367 Kennington Road
London SE11 4PT
Tel: 020 7840 9200
Fax: 020 7793 8484
Email: info@countryside-alliance.org
Web: www.countryside-alliance.org

The Game Conservancy Trust

Fordingbridge
Hampshire SP6 1EF
Tel: 01425 652381
Fax: 01425 651026
Email: info@gct.org.uk
Web: www.gct.org.uk

Index